PRICE OF WALES

PRICE OF WALES

GRAHAM PRICE

Written with Terry Godwin

WILLOW BOOKS
Collins
Grafton Street, London
1984

Willow Books
William Collins & Sons plc
London · Glasgow · Sydney
Auckland · Toronto · Johannesburg

First published in Great Britain 1984
© Terry Godwin

Price, Graham
Price of Wales
1. Price, Graham   2. Rugby football players
Wales–Biography
I. Title
796.33'3'0924   GV944.9.P/

ISBN 0 00 218066 9

Filmset in Linotron 202 Plantin
by Wyvern Typesetting Limited, Bristol
Printed and bound in Great Britain by
William Collins & Sons plc

Contents

Retirement

The history of rugby football is studded with examples of players whose careers have been cut short because of selectors' whims. Some have been forced from the limelight because of injury while others, such as Barry John, Gerald Davies and Gareth Edwards, didn't take any chances and made deliberate decisions to quit while at the top. I suppose I belong to the third category, having decided to retire when probably – though not certainly – I still had a few years left to rollick along the high road of international rugby. The chief difference from Barry, Gerald and Gareth, was that though I left the international scene for similar reasons, unlike them I wanted to carry on playing. My playing days for Wales may be over, but the enjoyment and satisfaction I derive from turning out for Pontypool, my club, will I hope, continue for many years to come. Consequently my career in rugby is not complete which I trust explains why I have chosen to start this story at the end of my international career rather than conform to the usual practice by beginning at the beginning.

It is also a matter of putting the record straight. For telling my side of the story behind my retirement. The uninformed revel in rumour and speculation and I suspect that when my decision was announced, all kinds of tales were put around – that I was suffering from a mysterious injury, or wanted to embarrass the selectors, or that I had cunningly avoided being thrown out anyway.

Although many things contributed to my decision, the chief reason I quit was that I was thoroughly fed up with the way the Welsh team was being run. I dislike incompetence of any kind. What was happening with the Welsh team appalled me, and with no channels open to express my opinion of the decline in the standard of selection, squad sessions and coaching, I resolved that the best thing to do was to inform the selectors that I was no longer available.

Playing for Wales was unquestionably the greatest thing in my life, an honour and pride in which I shall take to my grave. I may not express that pride as passionately as say, Ray Gravell, whose emotional outpourings leave no one in any doubt that he would die for his country. But my pride is no different; playing for my country was as profoundly important to me as it was to Gravell with all his strong chauvinism. Therefore to give it all up, never again to pull on that No. 3 jersey, and never again to experience the thrill of hearing 50,000 voices shouting 'Wales, Wales, Wales' at the Arms Park, was an enormous wrench, which hurts even now. That the wound was consciously self-inflicted must seem curious, if not perverse. Yet I have no doubt I did the right thing. The way things were, I felt I could not give my best because I could not commit myself to something I no longer enjoyed and which I believed was fundamentally the wrong method and approach towards producing the best XV in Wales. It was not a moral issue, more an awareness that there was not the slightest thing I could do to change the situation if I stayed. Indeed, by remaining in Wales's squad I might have compromised my belief that things had gone from bad to worse. It would have been completely dishonest to have made myself available for selection knowing that the choice of players and their preparation for international matches was a joke, and a bad one at that.

Playing international rugby has its pluses and its minuses just like everything in life. On the one hand, there is the honour, satisfaction, kudos, perks and popularity. On the other hand, are the sacrifices a player must make regarding his time and his personal life. In order to carry on playing, a player must be able to balance one against the other, and after nine seasons with the Welsh squad, with all its many demands in time and effort, it was clear that the scales were being tipped the wrong way. It no longer held the same attraction, or gave the same stimulation.

When I came back from the 1983 Lions tour of New Zealand, my desire to carry on playing for Wales was less than I expected. I returned with a groin injury, which meant a delayed start to the new season, but gave me the chance to consider objectively the preparations the other Welsh players were making for the Japanese match. I realised I didn't envy anyone their involvement; also it was pretty obvious that the manner of selection and the match policy were totally foreign to me. The seeds of doubt began to grow.

The prevalent view is that Wales, since, say 1979, have deteriorated because of the lack of quality players. Coaches and coaching have been criticised for producing players with little flair or expertise. While conceding that this may be partly true, I believe there were other critical factors.

Decision day for me was Saturday, 29 October 1983 after Pontypool had played Bridgend at the Brewery Field. Rhys Williams, one of the selectors, was at the match presumably to keep a watching brief on some of the players chosen for the Welsh squad to play Romania the following month. I was not in the squad, possibly because of doubts about my fitness, and because I had not played in many matches since resting after the Lions tour of New Zealand, one of the traditional 'perks' following a tour. Malcolm Lewis, of the WRU, had contacted me on behalf of the selectors to inquire about my availability. I told him I was fit and would be playing against Bridgend. To my mind, it was not a question of my fitness, but whether the selectors wanted me to play against Romania. In the event, I 'proved' myself against Bridgend, and Rhys Williams came up to me in the changing room after the match and told me to join the squad session the next day. I said that I'd be there. My answer was yes because Wales, it appeared, still wanted me, and I found the idea of playing behind the Iron Curtain for the first time quite attractive. Having settled that, I set about enjoying myself after a satisfying victory, hardly giving more than a passing thought to what I had agreed. I had a few beers, chatted with the Bridgend lads, and then moved on, as is Pontypool custom. On the way back to Pontypool, the team bus stopped at a pub near Cowbridge.

It was in this pub that I made the most momentous decision of my life – I was going to quit international rugby. Nothing was premeditated, it just happened. Jeff Squire, who unlike me, had been selected as an original member of the squad, sat next to me in the pub, and our discussion understandably centred upon the next day's squad session. Jeff was also less than happy about Sunday squad sessions and had for some time been considering giving up international rugby. His chief reason was, with increasing business commitments, he no longer had the time to devote to the demanding schedules playing for Wales involved. We both agreed that a squad session the day after a hard club match did not do us, or the Welsh teambuilding, any good whatsoever. Our doubts, mutually expressed, soon became conviction, and before we reboarded the team bus, we had agreed we'd call it a day at the same time. Perhaps we needed only a little push from each other to reach the decision which we had individually considered for some time: we were not going to attend the squad session the next day and we were not going to play for Wales again.

I think it is important to stress that originally I fully intended to go to the squad session. But the more I thought about it, the less I wanted to go through with it. When we sat talking after the Bridgend match, Jeff confided that he felt precisely the same way. We had often chatted about our dissatisfaction at the way the squad sessions were conducted; how the coaches had changed their opinions from those they had held during their playing days, particularly regarding fitness training, tactics and treatment of players during the squad sessions. It had been at times embarrassing, from Jeff's and my point of view, as well as by the squad supervisors themselves. Remember, we had all been team-mates at one time. Jeff actually went along to Cardiff to tell the selectors of his decision. He then left. I telephoned Rod Morgan, the chairman, to announce my decision after the squad session had finished. The double bombshell had fallen and it was left to a somewhat stunned press to pick up the pieces and chase both Jeff and me for the remainder of that Sunday in search of an explanation. To say that my telephone was red hot is an understatement. I had no time, or opportunity, to reflect on the decision, or to wonder whether it was the right or the wrong one. All I know is that once it was made public, I felt an enormous sense of relief that it was all over.

As I have already intimated, there were many reasons for my retirement. Taken separately they would perhaps not have justified it; together they made it inevitable. What many may not realise is that under different circumstances I may well have played on. My fitness and willingness to train would, I'm sure, have allowed me perhaps another five years in a Welsh jersey. Indeed, in many ways I was a far better player and just as fit, at 32 when I quit than when I first played for Wales. Some call it maturity, others experience. Whatever it may be, certainly it makes prop forwards last longer than any other position on the rugby field, and there was no reason to think I would have been an exception to the rule.

I would even go so far as to say I found propping easier at the end of my career and I am confident I could have done my job for Wales for, say, another 20 internationals. If the fitness, physical strength and commitment were there, unfortunately the will was not. Ambition, which had once burned brightly, had faded, and without it there was absolutely no way I could continue.

Ambition is the overdrive for all sportsmen. Without it, you will just plod along and end up with memories of what might have been. I was lucky that my ambition lasted as long as it did. I could hardly complain at what I had achieved: I was the most-capped Welsh forward of all time, most-capped Welsh prop, I had played – and been on a winning side – against every worth-while country, I had been on three Lions tours, had played in twelve consecutive tests for the Lions (more than any other Welshman), and had made more full international appearances than any other player in my position. I suppose I simply began to believe I had nothing else to prove . . . the hunger for more caps had been completely satisfied by the end of 1983.

Until I was dropped for the Scotland match early in 1983, all my caps had been successive which was very important to me. It's possible that if my run was still unbroken, I might have wanted to try to continue the sequence. Once the run was over, however, that particular aspiration died as well.

Being dropped also made me realise, for the first time, that perhaps there was more to life than playing for Wales. Although I was upset and annoyed at the way I had been treated by the selectors in this particular instance, I was surprised to find I didn't actually mind not playing at Murrayfield. It was the first time in nine seasons that I had not been involved with Wales and, in fact, I felt a sense of relief at not having to go through all the rigmarole of training sessions and the preparation for a big match. I watched the match live on television, another new experience, and I was pleased that the team won. Apart from that, it meant very little to me. This indifference, however, was momentary. Just as surely that my dropping had revealed feelings I didn't know I had, I quickly became determined to win back my place. It was a question of pride, rather than any significant change in attitude. The opportunity came in an unexpected way.

Ian Eidman, who had taken my place against Scotland, had played well enough to keep his place for the next international, against Ireland, to be played at Cardiff Arms Park. But early in the week of the match the rumours spread that Eidman was a doubtful starter because of a back injury. A couple of reporters, anticipating events, contacted me to inquire if I had been asked to replace Ian if he was unable to play. Apparently a television programme had hinted at the strong possibility. I got the impression that the reporters were fully expecting me to say that the selectors could 'stuff it'. Instead, I told them I knew nothing about Eidman's injury and had no idea who the selectors would call on to replace him.

It still came as a complete surprise when Clive Rowlands rang me at work to ask if I would play against Ireland because Eidman had failed a fitness test at the Thursday afternoon training session. My emotions at this sudden change in events were mixed. One thing I was sure of was that I wanted to make the most of this opportunity to play, for the first time in two or three years, with a pair of well-respected scrummagers in the second row – John Perkins and Bob Norster. I had a point to prove, to the selectors and to the public. Suffice to say our scrummaging was good, Ireland were comfortably beaten and I kept my place, on merit, for the last match of the 1983 campaign against France, which turned out to be my last match for Wales. None of this detracts from my views about the Sunday squads employed by the Welsh selectors, all day sessions that are demoralising, frustrating and, I believe, damaging to the Welsh cause.

A young player will sacrifice a great deal and give up all his free time in order to win his first cap. This enthusiasm is crucial if the player is going to keep his place. He therefore accepts the rigours of the squad sessions without complaint. However, the longer a player is part of the team, the more he realises that playing for his country is completely taking over his life, until he is enveloped by it. He is forced to live and breathe rugby. It is then that he begins to question the whole set-up. After all, rugby football is an amateur game, which, by its very nature is part-time. Yet the system seeks to professionalise everyone, in terms of time and commitment, which is grossly unfair. The Sunday squad, which often involves both morning and afternoon sessions, becomes a chore and the players rebel against it. On the one hand, the selectors implore players to cut down the amount of rugby they play because of the danger of becoming stale. On the other, they force the players to participate in what is equivalent to two matches on the day following a hard club match. Not even professional footballers, who are paid to play, would accept such conditions. If this happened only a couple of times in a season, perhaps it would not be so bad. But effectively, the leading Welsh players are now required to play, train and attend squad sessions, day in, day out for nearly the entire season. Most players have their own training schedules; all are required to train, practise and play for their clubs; the top players are then required by Wales. Such an exhausting regime is bound to sap players, to weaken their resolve and dampen their enthusiasm. It is not at all surprising that the Welsh team has not fulfilled its potential in recent years. Take, for example, the players involved in the two late 1983 matches against Japan and Romania, and the B match against France. These could hardly be described as top-class internationals, but by the end the players had surrendered nine consecutive Sundays to either preparation or match weekends.

It is not only the international set-up which suffers. The players' clubs, too, rarely get the best out of their star players, which they are entitled to, and club committees are often at a loss as to how they can rekindle enthusiasm. It is a vicious cycle, beneficial to no one, least of all to the most important people in the game, the players themselves. At the end of each season, a top Welsh player acts like a zombie, punch-drunk with playing and training. Our administrators tell us the game is fun, a pastime to be enjoyed. It may have been in their day. But then they did not have to experience anything like the demands, both physical and mental, made on the modern player.

Let me say at once that I considered myself more enthusiastic than most. Rugby meant a lot to me. I made the sacrifices willingly. But even my interest was dulled to the extent that by the end of the international season I would have been quite happy to throw my boots into the broom cupboard and forget about everything until the start of the new season. My attitude to club matches, too, suffered. I found I didn't want to play at all against such clubs as Penarth and Abertillery. I was even indifferent to the 'big ones', against Cardiff, Bridgend, Newport and Llanelli, which used to get the adrenalin flowing, but which often I treated merely as routine matches. This was wrong and unfair to myself and to Pontypool. I realised why it had happened and what had to be done: I would have to sacrifice my place in the squad.

If I reiterate the view that the totalitarian methods adopted by Wales have been the cause of the decline of our game, it is intended not so much as confirmation of my own frustration, but more in the hope that someone might take notice and look for alternatives. I do not subscribe to the view that we have lacked quality players. What I will say is that we have not had enough quality selectors. The real weakness of the selectors since 1979 is not that many of them wouldn't know a good player when they saw one, but that they often negate all their efforts, good and bad, by playing people out of position. Fundamentally this is bad practice, in the same way as one rotten apple in the barrel ruins all. To pick someone to play, for example, at centre when he has played solely at fly-half will work only if that player is exceptionally gifted (and there aren't many of those around). More often than not, it is unfair on the player concerned because he will be unable to do himself justice because he is asked to do a job for which he is neither skilled nor experienced. He will become a burden on the rest of the team, as they will be prevented from playing to their full potential. At international level, it is absolutely essential that every player does his own job well. A player struggling out of position often needs the help of others, who are thus unable to concentrate on their own jobs. It is fairly obvious that the best way a player can help his team-mates is to do his own job competently. Wales, too often, played men unable to do this. It was not their fault.

The prime example of such bad selection was Richard Moriarty, of Swansea. In Moriarty's case the selectors slipped up not once but twice. If Moriarty has a place at international level, it would have to be at No. 8, a position for which his size, pace and mobility qualifies him. But what did Wales do? At first they played him at lock forward, overlooking the fact that the basic requirement for that position, above all, is to be able to scrummage and scrummage hard. When Moriarty, ultimately, was found wanting as a lock, he was dropped. His recall, to play at blind-side flanker against Scotland in 1984, emphasised once again the selectors' ignorance of the requirements of the position. Moriarty floundered like a fish out of water, simply because he did not possess the qualities of a blind-side flanker. Had Moriarty been the only choice for the position, there would have been some excuse for the gamble. But there was no shortage of specialised blind-side flankers in Wales and I could have named as many as four players who would have constituted better selection. You can only imagine their resentment when they were overlooked in favour of someone with absolutely no track record in the position. Such resentment, of course, is another example of the gulf between players and selectors which has widened in recent years, and is hardly conducive to producing a healthy and happy squad system, which is another ingredient necessary to produce a successful international XV.

Apart from the increasing commitment required by squad sessions, another worrying development has been the intrusion into players' private lives. An amateur player is more entitled to privacy than a professional one, and to put pressure on him in this way is both unfair and unrealistic. I believe that for an amateur, fitness is essentially a personal thing and it should be left to the individual. However, today's Welsh squad player is forced to adopt a fitness training schedule, which if strictly followed, entails the loss of almost all his spare time that he should be spending with his family or pursuing other interests. This schedule is ridiculous. Devised by fitness experts Tom Hudson and Dr Bruce Davies, the schedule embraces every week of the season and basically recommends four training sessions lasting one and a half hours each, or a total of six hours a week. Six hours a week does not sound a great deal, until one adds on the time required for travelling, changing and showering. The schedule, remember, is on top of the player's club requirements and his own fitness programme. Effectively, a player is required to commit himself to rugby, one way or another, six days a week every week of the season! We were told that the schedule was merely a recommendation and was not compulsory.

This is just another example of Welsh selectors' doublethink. Why on earth introduce it, if it was not intended to be adhered to. Players are entitled to ask if those who authorised such a demanding training regime would have followed it themselves? As I have already said, an amateur player's fitness is a personal thing – he will already be making sacrifices on his own time as he thinks appropriate. How much work it is depends on the individual and his own ambitions. If a player isn't prepared to commit himself, then he doesn't deserve to get on and realise his ambitions. But it is his decision, and always must be. I remember having an argument with John Bevan after the Wales–Maoris match. I told him it was demanding too much of amateur players to subject them to fitness tests and to expect them to train according to the fitness schedules. They were not adopted during the period when Wales won two Grand Slams and four consecutive Triple Crowns and therefore cannot be necessary now. All the fitness testing did not help Wales in their draw against England, or their struggle against Japan or their thrashing from Romania or their losing at home to Scotland and France.

The straw that broke this particular back, finally, was the attitude adopted at the squad sessions. In recent years, the players have been treated like schoolboys by the organisers, particularly the coaches, Bevan and Cobner. No grown man with any self-respect will allow himself to be shouted at, sometimes ridiculed, jeered at and generally treated as if he were a complete idiot. For some of the players, particularly the young and unsuspecting, the treatment was accepted without protest. For others, like myself and the other older, more experienced players, it was embarassing and insulting. After all, those barking out the orders were men with whom we had played. This in itself demanded respect, sympathy and understanding. None of this was evident or forthcoming. I don't think I made my resentment at such treatment clear, but instead disguised my unhappiness behind my usual inscrutable scowl. I was later to learn that some of the selectors were anxious to quash the 'rebellion' (which of course it never was), and the best way to do it was to throw out the culprits. I had the distinct impression that neither Jeff Squire nor me were wanted in the Championship squad in 1983, and that any excuse would be found to drop us. What we had to contribute as players was not important, all that mattered was that we represented a challenge to the system and therefore had to go. I suppose Jeff and I survived so long because of the problems in replacing us and also the difficulty in justifying our omission.

For anyone outside the game, it may be difficult to understand the politics and pressures which are an integral part of international rugby. When these pressures become overwhelming you cannot relax and enjoy playing as you would wish to, and the situation is not helped by the growing tendency of the critics to treat rugby as a professional game. Players at the top are regarded as professional and are now expected to adopt a professional attitude. Although this is obviously untrue – rugby union players are not paid to play – the consequences of such treatment are far-reaching. The pressure is expressed in different ways: players become over-concerned about making mistakes as they realise that their mistakes will be highlighted by television and the newspapers: action replays might be fascinating for the journalist and the public, but for the player it might mean they are dropped from the team. The players' response to such close examination is understandable: they make extra efforts to eliminate the kind of errors which could be the subject of media scrutiny, which in turn unavoidably leads to less attractive rugby, that again being criticised. Players have become prisoners of the system. You wonder where it is all going to end.

Such were my reasons for retiring from international rugby. I have no regrets, for I achieved far more than I ever dreamed possible when I first played for Wales in 1975. Although the latter part of my career was not as stimulating or as enjoyable as the early successes, I prefer to remember that the good times far outweighed the disappointments and the frustrations. For that I am truly grateful.

The Early Days

One of these days, perhaps when my playing days are over, I intend to visit Egypt and take in, like every good tourist should, the Pyramids, the Sphinx, the Nile and the Valley of the Kings. This is not because I have a particularly strong desire to see them but more out of a natural curiosity to see the country in which I was born.

Not that I learnt very much about Egypt or its culture. I was born in Moascar, 100 miles from Cairo, on 24 November 1951, but was there only two months which understandably didn't leave much time to get to know the country, the people or the sights. Nor did such a short stay really entitle me to claim – as has been suggested later in my life – dual nationality. We were a services family. My father was a sergeant major in the RAOC, and Egypt was one of his many overseas postings. If that removes all doubts about my birthright, there can be none about my nationality: my father was from Carno in Montgomeryshire and my mother was Rhondda-born and bred, from Treorchy to be precise.

After leaving Egypt, we lived at Blackpool, Corsham and Bicester. I was six when the family settled in Pontypool, my father leaving the Army after 30 years to become a policeman at the nearby Royal Ordnance Factory at Glascoed. I did not know it then, of course, but my Pontypool Connection had started. Not that rugby featured in my early life – which was hardly surprising because my father was much more interested in hockey and football, sports which he had been good at when he was young.

My first real contact with the 'other game', in an organised sense, was when I became a pupil, at the age of 11, at West Mon

GS in Pontypool, a school with a tradition for producing first-class rugby players. Like most Welsh boys of my age, however, the rudiments of the game had been gleaned a little earlier in the rough-and-tumble with local lads in a field near our house at Glascoed. We were lucker than most in that we were able to play with a proper leather ball. An aunt had given it to me after winning it in a raffle. When new the ball was covered with the autographs of many different sportsmen. After a few sessions in the mud and rain, they were soon obliterated. So much for youthful disregard of the famous. I can't even remember whose signatures I had. I never dreamed that, one day, I would be asked to sign balls in the same way.

Rugby was a far more serious affair at West Mon, and by the time I was 15 I knew much more about the game. The only position I had not been tried out in was full-back. This was not so much a mark of outstanding versatility as of expedience. If we were short of a player in the pack, or the backs, usually I was the one selected. I was a comparatively strong runner with the ball in hand, which was probably why Max Horton, our PE teacher and rugby coach at West Mon, considered my future lay at centre, a position I enjoyed and at which I did fairly well for the school. However, the organisers of the district representative side – the Pontypool & Blaenavon Schools – were not so convinced. They tried me at centre, flank and lock in a trial – and then with bewildering eccentricity they picked me to play prop for my first representative appearance, against Cwmbran Schools. This was in the 1966–67 season. My future was determined, though I didn't realise it then.

The following year I went straight into West Mon's 1st XV at loose-head prop, and, having become used to and more experienced in that position, I became a candidate for Welsh Schools. In 1968–69 I played in two WSSRU Under 19 matches, against Yorkshire and Welsh Youth, and the following year I played in five internationals, against England at Bristol, France at Llanelli, Scotland at Murrayfield, Welsh Youth at Swansea and Yorkshire at Newport. Interestingly, we lost only to the Welsh Youth, who at the time were very strong with players like Hefin Jenkins, Glyn Shaw and Ray Gravell. Even now, I remember them as very hard matches. Not that the Welsh Schools were without talent. During my first season, I played with Robin Williams, John Bevan, even then a power-ful, strong-running wing, and Brynmor Williams. The next season my colleagues included Brynmor again, Richard Barrel, Steve Lewis, Jeff Herdman, Stuart Lane and Alun Meredith. Clive Rees, I remember, was a reserve.

My last schools' representative match, against Yorkshire, is of special memory because of a try which in many ways resembled the one I scored for Wales on my international début in 1975. Yorkshire threw in long at a line-out, we won the ball, peeled, and I instigated a passing movement from inside our own 25-yard area. I was still there, at hand, to take the final pass after we had swept the whole length of the field.

Rugby was not my only interest at school. I was quite keen on athletics, without ever being a very serious competitor, which was probably why I tried my hand at most disciplines, from sprints to field events. I was fortunate in being naturally strong and fast, but it was not until my final two years at West Mon that I concentrated on the shot and discus. The school did not organise many competitions, however, and my athletic development was limited to the school's sports and the county championships. The standard, admittedly, was not very high, which was probably why in 1970 I was able to win the Welsh Schools shot and discus titles. In fact, that season I competed only six times, which included a four-nation international against Ireland, England and Scotland in Dublin. Wales did not exactly set the athletics world on fire, but interestingly on that Dublin trip were two other future British Lions, Brynmor Williams, who was selected for the high jump, and Clive Rees in the sprints.

Although by the age of 18 I had decided I wanted to become an engineer, I didn't have the necessary academic qualifica-tions. A year at Alsager Training College was therefore more of a compromise rather than any great desire to become a teacher. Alsager, however, enabled me to gain more rugby experience –

they even tried me out as a place kicker on occasions. Colin McFadyean, the England threequarter, was a lecturer at Alsager but we saw very little of him apart from the odd coaching session. I remember Colin best for his instruction in life-saving techniques at Crewe Baths. These included jumping 30 feet from the top board and fanning out like a skydiver just before hitting the water. That jump was not designed to make McFadyean the most popular man at Alsager, I can tell you.

Having failed to make a Chris Snode out of yours truly, Alsager turned their attention to trying to turn me into a decathlete. Daley Thompson need not have lost any sleep. Although I satisfied the athletics coach, Harry Mawdsley, by my competence in some of the disciplines (I was good enough, for instance, to win the Monmouthshire Senior shot and discus, that year), I came down to earth, literally, in the pole vault. Only a few of us were allowed to use the bridging pole, a kind of semi-flexible pole. My instructions were straightforward: run as fast as I could on the approach and then plant the pole securely in the box. The pole, I was assured, would bend, and all I needed to do then was to swing with it and I would be catapulted upwards and over the bar. So much for theory. Fast I ran, the pole went into the box, and sure enough I was catapulted – not upwards and over, but backwards some 30 feet to crash on to the cinders. Winded and wiser, the decision was taken then and there to leave the decathlon to Daley Thompson.

By this time, too, I had decided that I had been a bachelor long enough. I had met Anne in 1970, when I was 18 and still at school. Our first brief encounter was rather more Michael Green than Barbara Cartland – we met at the Pontypool Rugby Club's annual dinner. Anne's father was secretary of the Pontypool RFC Social Club, and her grandfather, Sammy Lloyd, had been the club trainer for 40 years. In other words, Anne was a member of one of the great Pontypool family dynasties. She had been going to the club since she was four, and she has missed the annual dinner only once since she first attended as an eleven-year-old. We were married on Sunday, 8

August 1971, at St Luke's Church, Pontwenynydd, a little over a month after I had ended my brief association with Alsager College. We now have three children, Louise, Joanne and Owen. I haven't made up my mind what position Owen will play. Anne is certain of one thing, though, he's going to be a Pontypool player!

As a newly married man, I needed to earn a living and for two years I worked as a laboratory technician in the chemical department of Parke-Davis in Pontypool. During the next three years, however, it was back to studying. I took a National Diploma in building construction at Nash College, Newport and read civil engineering at UWIST, Cardiff. While all this was happening, of course, my rugby career was also developing. I was still a student at UWIST when I went on my first British Lions tour to New Zealand in 1977. So much had happened since it had all begun with my kicking around that autographed rugby ball on a Glascoed field . . .

Ray Prosser

I think most sportsmen would readily admit that one person was either instrumental in altering the course of their career or was a major influence on it. In my case, that person was Ray Prosser, and it was one of the luckiest events of my life that we met. Of course it was entirely fortuitous but sometimes I would rather like to think it may have been preordained. Whether it was destiny or accident our paths crossed at a crucial time for both of us – I was 17, raw and inexperienced, and Prosser, his notable playing career over, was anxious to make his mark as a coach.

The meeting point, of course, was Pontypool Rugby Club. The year was 1970, when Pontypool was nowhere near the great club it now is, and often suffered the kind of hammerings endured today by poor Penarth. It may be something of an understatement to say that we both started at the bottom. There was nowhere else for Pontypool, Prosser and me to go but up. Naturally, after leaving school, I was eager to join a club. With no ties or links with any particular club, I was open to persuasion. The offer which I could not refuse came from Max Horton, a Pontypool selector, who asked if I was interested in 'a game or two' for the Athletic, Pontypool's second team. I am not exactly renowned for quick verbal responses; but on this occasion I leapt at the chance, and in due course, I played for the Athletic against Monmouth at Pontypool Park. This was Easter, 1969, and having enjoyed the experience, I was more than willing to strengthen the association by training with Pontypool throughout the summer. Injuries over the Christmas period gave me the chance of my first team début – against, of all people, Gloucester. However, it was towards the end of the same season that the Pontypool committee made what was to prove one of the most momentous decisions in the club's history – they appointed Prosser coach.

I can't describe the respect or rather awe, I felt for Big Ray. One of the great forwards of all time, he was a hearty, powerful man whose career had been forged in the furnaces of countless internationals and who, off the field, was renowned for being one of the characters of Welsh rugby. I was doubtful, to put it mildly, as to how I would measure up to the great man's high standards. I soon discovered that Pross, as he was affectionately known, had just one formula for a successful rugby player – and that was work, work and even more work. If I have given the impression of a heartless slave-driver, I must temper it by stating that he would never ask anyone to do anything which he had not already done himself – and I think that contains a moral for a coach at any level of the game. I learned, too, that Pross would persevere with a young player and push him to the limits only if he considered the player had potential. Quite simply, if Prosser did not believe a player could make it to the top, he would simply leave him to his own devices. This was not so much cold-shouldering a player with limited ability, as aiming at excellence with those who Prosser believed were capable of helping him to produce a side to match and conquer any team in the land.

It may have seemed harsh to some, but as a youngster I accepted the philosophy totally. Now, nearly 15 years later, Pross – and Pontypool – have proved the point. The Prosser philosophy was, and remains, a good one. I was happy to be driven non-stop by Pross in training. It was not – for me, at least – a grinding, monotonous method simply to obtain maximum fitness but a necessity if one believed, as I did, that it would help me realise my ambition to play international rugby. Pross's belief in hard work was, of course, only part of the preparation: it was – and still is – an education in itself to listen and learn from his experiences, and to realise that he was one of the rare breed who could assess objectively the strengths and weaknesses of every player in the side. A man with an agile mind, a sharp tongue and, a wicked sense of humour, he had us laughing our heads off one moment and hating his guts the next – that curious formula which inspires not resentful disagreement but deference and respect.

Another important lesson of that early tuition was that he insisted I should concentrate on what I was good at, and that I should always aim for perfection. 'If you don't give it everything you've got, it's not the team you are cheating on, it's yourself', was another of Prosser's pronouncements which rings loud and clear in my ears even now. Such a demand for commitment may sound pretty obvious, but I have known players, well-known ones at that, who would not only disagree with it, but wouldn't even begin to understand it.

It may come as a surprise to some, but Pross also quickly dismissed any illusions I may have had about becoming a running prop, lithe and agile, galloping in for tries and trying to catch people's attention in open play. 'I don't care what you do about the field', Pross declared; 'Just do your job as a prop in the scrum and I'll be satisfied.' He required me to be a committed, hard-working scrummager, believing rightly that my enjoyment would chiefly come from being a specialist and doing the job well. Pross's hard unrelenting attitude has never changed. No matter how well we played – or thought we had played – if, for example, we lost a ball on our own put-in, he would remember this 'sin', lecture us unmercifully, and wouldn't let us forget it for at least a week. On the other side of the coin, if any of us was criticised in the press, he would be the first to tell us if he thought the criticism unjustified.

When I first joined Pontypool I played at loose-head prop, but switched to the tight-head when Charlie Faulkner joined us from Cross Keys. Soon after, Bobby Windsor arrived to complete one partnership that was to become famous as the Pontypool Front Row. I'm continually asked the secret of the Pontypool Front Row's success but I find it very difficult to answer. What I can say is that we hit it off immediately as a partnership and the combination worked well. We got on well with each other, and the ever-present Ray Prosser was continually urging and pressing us for better performances.

We played our first match together for Wales, against France, in 1975 and we played together in 19 internationals. It could have been more, but for the fact that Charlie found himself out of favour and was then injured in 1977, when he missed four internationals.

At first, we were a bit embarrassed to say the least, by the publicity the Pontypool Front Row received, particularly after Max Boyce wrote 'Up and Under' about us. When eventually we became used to it we realised that it was much more of a tribute to Prosser than to us. He had welded us together just as he had the rest of the Pontypool pack. Pross, as I have said, was a man of many skills and I suspect he knew that we would become a good unit before Bobby and Charlie joined me at Pontypool. I've since found out that Pross always knows if there is a player around whom he wants, and usually he succeeds in getting his man. This is not to suggest that Pross was Pontypool's only talent scout. Players, particularly the senior ones, were on the look-out for promising players to join Pontypool.

A good example of this was Jeff Squire. Jeff was unhappy at Newport and we at Pontypool were not alone in thinking that potentially he was a far better player. We had played with and against him, and while it may not always suit us to say so, players know the capabilities of other players better than anyone.

We did not have any Master Plan to trap Squire, but he could have been forgiven for thinking that he had been ensnared by co-ordinated effort on our part! The ambush was set in Australia, during the Welsh tour of 1978, when the Pontypool representation somewhat outnumbered that of Newport's: apart from myself, we had Bobby Windsor, Charlie Faulkner and Terry Cobner, while the Rodney Paraders had only two tourists, Gareth Evans and Squire himself. Fortunately, Bobby Windsor was given the job of allocating the rooms to the players, so it was not altogether surprising when Squire found himself 'doubled up' with Pontypool players only. Bobby began the bombardment, and gave Jeff quite an ear-bashing, telling him what a great club Pontypool was, what a fantastic coach Ray Prosser was, and how much Jeff's playing would improve if he joined us. Every club has its own particular strategy for luring players to its ranks. None, I think, had a maestro to equal Bobby Windsor, who I'm sure could persuade Ken Livingstone to join the Tory Party.

Squire, inevitably, succumbed although I suspect that after Bobby, then Charlie and Terry, by the time it came to my turn he had already been completely worn down, all resistance gone! On our return from Australia Squire had made up his mind to switch from black and amber to red, black and white. Jeff must have wondered whether he'd made the right decision, because after Bobby and the rest of us, he came face to face with Prosser, who after an initial warm, sincere welcome, proceeded to give him the Pontypool treatment: Squire worked harder in training than he ever had at Newport. At first Jeff struggled to cope with the new regime. But soon he too understood the value of 100 per cent preparation and, mesmerised by the Prosser magic, he became a new man able, like me, to claim that Prosser is responsible for his position in the rugby world.

Had I joined any club other than Pontypool, it is conceivable that I might have won a few Welsh caps. But without Prosser's influence, I'm sure I would not have become Wales's record cap holder or gone on three Lions tours. Unquestionably, I owe all that to Ray Prosser. He might argue that I was part of a partnership. I've heard that Pross has said that Graham Price above all else is a Pontypool man. I will not disagree with that. His philosophy is that given the right material and willing co-operation of the player involved, he can turn a good forward into a great one. That is Pontypool tradition, and the person who established it was Pross. Where backs are concerned – 'they'm prima donnas', as he calls them – Prosser believes they have to be natural players, and they are allowed to do their own thing without too much interference from him.

Some people, many of whom should know better, have criticised Prosser for turning Pontypool into a ten-man team and accused him of not being interested in the back-line. It is not out of loyalty to Prosser that I totally refute such criticism. I prefer to use facts to back up my argument: for instance, during each of the last ten years we have scored as many tries as most clubs, often more, and on numerous occasions our wings, like Goff Davies, David Hussey and Steve Evans, have been the club's leading try scorers. Which meant, occasionally, they were also the leading try scorers in Wales. Similarly, our scrum-halves, like Nigel Osborne and David Bishop, have topped all try-scoring records, and one season Osborne and Evans were the top two in Wales. Those, I would suggest, are hardly the statistics of a side exclusively devoted to ten-man rugby.

Another accusation which angers me, is that after Pontypool perfected the rolling maul, they then proceeded to bore everyone to death with it. To suggest this is to completely misunderstand Prosser's attitude. Improvisation and variety are his catchwords, and often he would tell us to go out and forget the maul and switch to rucking. This was because he had analysed the maul better than anyone else: he saw that we had occasionally become undisciplined, had become too loose and were 'rolling' and supporting simply for the sake of it. Prosser was also the first coach in Wales to develop the eight-man drive on the opposition's line on every occasion. Once again Pontypool were criticised for consistently using this ploy, although I've now been on two Lions tours when we employed identical tactics.

I've trained under some of the best coaches in the world, and discussed with many others the techniques and tactics of the modern game. There is no doubt in my mind that when it comes to forward play Ray Prosser has no equal. He has turned countless good players into very good ones and when you look at the number of internationals he has helped to produce, it reads like a Welsh *Who's Who*: apart from myself, Charlie Faulkner and Bobby Windsor, the list includes Eddie Butler, Terry Cobner, Jeff Squire, Staff Jones, John Perkins, Mark Brown and Steve Sutton. Unintentionally, of course, it represents a whole pack plus two, and by any standards, it is an incredible achievement for one man. Rugby football is Prosser's life. It is all he thinks about and I'll bet it's all he dreams about. I know he was deeply hurt when he was voted off the Pontypool committee in the days before he became coach, and I am sure he still bears a grudge against those who voted him off.

But I also know that when we beat Swansea so convincingly to win the Welsh Cup in 1983, it was one of the proudest moments of his life. It was the only occasion when I have seen him struggle to hold back the tears . . . at last his beloved Pontypool had proved themselves unquestionably the best club in the country. It will be a moment he will savour for the rest of his life, and I am sure there wasn't one player who did not feel great pride that he had played a part in giving Pross his moment of glory.

It has been a popular misconception that Prosser had ambitions higher than being just Pontypool coach. The truth is that he never wanted, for instance, to be Wales's coach – even if they had asked him. Curiously enough, though Prosser is the best coach of forwards in the world, he still hasn't passed the Welsh Rugby Union's written examination for coaches. And it's not because the WRU have not wanted him to be 'qualified'. Many times, he was invited to participate in the two-week long Welsh Coaching Course held in Aberystwyth so that he could receive his certificate. Prosser always refused. This caused some consternation and, of course, embarrassment to the WRU who understandably wanted all senior Welsh coaches to carry their seal of approval. They shortened the course's length to a weekend for him – then it became a day, then half an hour. Still Prosser held out. He regarded the certificate as nothing more than a piece of paper, but probably his refusal was based on the fact that there was little point in his attending a course where he could learn nothing. It would have been like asking a mathematics professor to go back to school to learn his ten times tables.

I suspect that the course organisers might have found themselves learning from Prosser – one wonders whether they could have passed his examination! Henry Cooper used to have difficulty in finding and keeping sparring partners because he would not pull his punches. Ray Prosser is precisely the same. He speaks his mind, regardless of the consequences. He has the straightforward honesty of the ordinary man, which he is proud to be, and he cares little that some regard him as blunt and tactless. You have to take Pross as you find him, which for most people means a warm, totally sincere person, but one who is intolerant of hypocrisy or rugby men who know nothing of the finer points of the game. That withering look and abrupt, caustic comment have shrivelled many.

This leads me to Barry John. I have no wish to tarnish the reputation of one of Welsh rugby's immortals and one of the most accomplished fly-halves the world has known. But when Barry John took it on himself to describe Pontypool as: 'a cancer on Welsh rugby', B.J. could hardly have expected to win any friends at Pontypool Park. By that one tactless statement he criticised our club, and by implication, one of the world's greatest rugby thinkers, so he has set himself apart. For some at Pontypool the remark was tantamount to a demand for the reintroduction of capital punishment. As far as I, and many others are concerned, B.J. has lost friendship, respect and credibility.

I was not present when John levelled his infamous charge at Eddie Butler, after Wales had been defeated by Romania in Bucharest on 12 November 1983. I'm sure Butler, an old hand at rebuffing outrageous prejudice and criticism, dealt adequately with the situation. According to Eddie, B.J.'s remarks were made in a 'real ding-dong' of a discussion, which was overheard by several Welsh supporters. One of these, who described himself as a friend of Barry John, actually wrote to Eddie later, apologising for the outburst. 'There is no way I could condone what he said', the writer declared. Butler was also reasonably sure that B.J.'s obvious dislike of Pontypool dated from a match he played at Pontypool Park years ago, when he was clouted. It must have been a really good one for him to remember it all these years later, but obviously not good enough to have knocked any sense into him. His 'cancer' declaration was irresponsible and unfounded. I presume he was referring to Pontypool's forward-based style of play. He is not alone in having no knowledge of what the game is all about; his dislike of the way we play at Pontypool, however, is curious for I don't think we have seen very much of him in recent seasons. That is undoubtedly his loss, not ours. He might have learned a few things about rugby, not the least of which is that we are a club which plays to its strengths. These happen to be in the forwards, and the fact that we can play seven full internationals, five of whom are British Lions, confirms that some, at least, have a higher opinion of our ability than B.J. Would he rather we didn't play to our forward strength? That would be like having asked Llanelli not to play to their threequarters strength when B.J. was playing for them. Llanelli are renowned for their backs. Pontypool are famed for their forwards. Llanelli, I'm sure, would have been delighted to have had our forwards as well. Similarly, Pontypool would have been proud to have had Llanelli's backs when they were at their prime.

Much has been said and written about Pontypool's negative tactics. I'm not exactly sure what these are – it can't be negative to want to win a match, it is positive. It is not negative to want to win as much possession as possible, which is the basic idea behind all coaching of skill and technique. It is not negative to use the possession in the best way possible, which is to gain ground and score points. This is what Pontypool do. They set out to win in a positive, planned way, which is no different from any side for whom I have played, whether it is county, Wales or the Lions. The strategy and tactics have always been the same: to play to the forwards early on, to control play and score a few points in order to set a platform on which to build and even bigger victory. It is successful, winning rugby, and for Barry John to criticise it is absurd considering that when he played for Wales and the Lions he was part of precisely the same strategy. Has he forgotten 1971 in New Zealand? The tactics which won the series included B.J. making full use of the forwards' hard-won possession, which meant he often had to kick. For a so-called running fly-half, was that kicking negative? Of course not. I'll bet that B.J. kicked far more often in the Tests in New

Zealand than our current fly-half, Mike Goldsworthy, does in ordinary club matches.

Until recently, Pontypool were not blessed with outstanding backs. Llanelli, for example, have found themselves in the reverse position, for they seem to attract ready-made players, such as schools or youth internationals. That is their good fortune, but they have had bad luck with their forwards. Both clubs, however, play to win, for that is what it is all about at top level. I am not saying that before Pross established himself, we weren't a little dull. But nowadays Pontypool play the most expansive 15-man game in Welsh rugby. We are exciting to watch, and we score tries, often many more than clubs which Barry John rates higher. Some clubs run the ball all afternoon and get thrashed in the process. That is not rugby, and never will be. If we have influenced Welsh rugby in the last 15 years, it has been to the good. We have provided Wales with forwards who do their job, which is to win the ball so that the backs can run, kick and score points to the best of their ability. Are Pontypool to be blamed if Wales have not always possessed top-quality backs? I hardly think so. If you have high-class threequarters, naturally you employ them to the full. If not, you must adopt a different approach. But, for heaven's sake, do not blame Pontypool because Welsh rugby strategy has lost its direction in recent years. I would even go so far as to say that had Wales adopted Pontypool's style and approach, they would have been much more successful 1979–84. It is a pity that Barry John has not had the sense to recognise our worth or understand our contribution.

As far as I know, Ray Prosser has not responded to B.J.'s accusation. I don't think he will. He has no need to prove he knows more about rugby football than any prima donna – Barry John included. One final comment: 'Pontypool thoroughly deserved this victory over arch rivals Newport. Their magnificent forwards laid the foundations of success. Their performance in the opening 30 minutes was near exhibition class . . .' This report appeared in the *Daily Express* on 14 September 1972. The author of the piece was Barry John.

Barry John does not stand alone in the firing squad. Mervyn Davies and Peter Walker frequently make allusions to Pontypool when the subject of foul play is discussed in Wales. Mervyn has made several spiteful comments about Welsh rugby in the *Daily Mirror* such as, 'I hope England give Wales a hiding', but he saves his most caustic remarks for Pontypool. Ex-cricketer Walker, who writes for a Sunday newspaper, seems to choose his words more carefully. However, the end result is the same – a condemnation of the way that Pontypool allegedly conduct themselves on the rugby field.

You would suppose that both are familiar with the way we play. I find this puzzling, for it is a rare occurrence – if ever at all – for either to be seen, in any capacity, at Pontypool Park or any other ground at which we play. Presumably the only time they see Pontypool in action is when matches are televised and shown in an edited 20 minutes on a Sunday afternoon. Messrs Davies and Walker may have found it disconcerting that the three matches in which Pontypool were televised (against Bridgend, Llanelli and Cardiff) in the 1983–84 season were among the most exciting and highly acclaimed of the season. In each Pontypool played in a manner no different to any when David Parry-Jones and the BBC cameras were elsewhere.

Mervyn seems to have conveniently forgotten his playing days, particularly when he was captain of Wales and the pack leader of forwards, several of whom came from Pontypool. They stood by him on the international field and didn't let him down. Moreover, his pre-match team talks to the forwards were little different, about motivation and the manner of playing, from any other pack leader with whom I have played. Unquestionably he then accepted that a certain amount of physical intimidation is part of a side's approach. If it was the norm then, why should anything be different now, as far as Mervyn is concerned?

I also do not understand why Walker takes Pontypool to task. It's possible that he cannot differentiate between a hard, physical approach and foul play. But it seems to me a gross hypocrisy that, for instance, Walker should regard Frank

'Typhoon' Tyson so highly, a tremendously fast bowler who occasionally resorted to bodyline bowling. In an interview in the *Western Mail*, Walker described Tyson's bowling as: 'The batsman went through a fifth of a second's terror before he hit the ball or the ball hit him.' If that does not accurately describe physical intimidation, then what does? It is sheer duplicity to defend foul play in a game such as cricket which is supposed to be an activity involving a lot less physical contact than rugby.

There must have been a lot of gleeful hand rubbing and pencil sharpening when Bristol decided to terminate fixtures with Pontypool towards the end of the 1984 season. Here again, roared our critics, was another example of unacceptable behaviour on the field. It was strange that the reporters who covered the match which led to the rift with Bristol, tried to defend us and our play when Bristol cancelled fixtures. Let me say immediately that Bristol had no grounds, in terms of dirty play, for ending fixtures. It was a hard match but contained nothing to justify the split. What indeed did Bristol make of two other leading English clubs, Sale and Coventry, coming to our defence and complimenting us on our attitude and style of play. My own view is that Bristol, for totally unrelated reasons, wanted to stop playing Pontypool and they tried to justify their decision by accusing us of malpractice. It's possible that Bristol are not prepared to accept the harder, physical approach that is part of our game. To be fair to them, I don't think I'd relish the prospect of travelling long distances to away matches in mid-week, playing a demanding, physical match against one of Britain's top sides and then having to return home in the early hours with the thought of having to get up to go to work. If I remember correctly, a couple of Bristol players spoke out against this policy earlier in the season. Perhaps this played a part. If that was the case, it is not Pontypool's approach which is at fault, but that of fixture secretaries who inflict match after match on players without any consideration.

In the 1972–73 season, when playing for Pontypool at Bristol, I broke through from a line-out but was then obstructed by one of the Bristol props, who grabbed my arm. I turned and tried to free myself when another Bristol forward, not involved in the action, threw a punch which fractured my cheekbone. As a result of that injury, I not only missed a month of the season, but had to drop out of the Gwent side to play the All Blacks. I didn't complain, Pontypool didn't protest and so the incident was not publicised. In view of the way Pontypool are treated nowadays, perhaps we should have complained. We might even get some sympathy, who knows?

I have no doubt that Prosser's one and only concern is for the players. Sometimes he loves us all like sons. On other occasions he can't even remember our names, which is precisely why he always gives a player a nickname as soon as he joins the Pontypool squad. His sense of humour is legendary, of course, but it is underrated when it comes to handing out nicknames. For example, I was 'Lionhead' for a long time. I don't know whether I was thus distinguished because I had played for the Lions or whether he thought I looked like one. Before 'Lionhead' I was 'Pimplehead', which I endured from the time I joined the club as a spotty-faced schoolboy. Bobby Windsor likewise suffered many names, but 'Bobby the Bolt' has stood the longest test. Because Eddie Butler went to university, he is called 'Bamber', or sometimes 'Educated Edward'. Staff Jones is simply called 'Fat Ass', and I presume he will be stuck with that for life. Our training sessions, as I have indicated are no laughing matter, but we all fell about on one occasion when Mark Brown, our 6 feet 4 inches coloured flanker, became 'Shaft', and you don't have to be a detective to know where Pross dug up that one. The ultimate Prosser insult fell on a young scrum-half, who never quite made it as a player. Not only did Pross fail to remember his name but was at a loss to think up a nickname for him: 'Whatever your f...... name is, you're doing it all wrong,' he shouted.

Keith Masters, one of our wings, wears a hearing-aid and naturally he was dubbed 'Deafy'. Masters was one of the few to get back at Pross when, subjected to a pretty steady flow of verbal abuse during training, he retorted: 'There's no need to shout, Pross, I can't hear you anyway'.

There are others, of course. Our hooker Steve Jones is 'Aubrey' (but we can't talk about that in this book!), Goff Davies is 'Sheets', Martin Jones is 'Horsehead', Chris Huish is 'Madman', John Perkins is 'Perky', Haydn (Morton) is 'Lumphead'. The list goes on and on. Most are self-explanatory, inventions of Prosser's impish humour. Some were needful of elucidation, Pross decided. Peter Lewis, a GP, earned what seemed a pretty mundane and obvious pet name of 'Doc'. 'It's after Dr Doolittle' explained Pross, 'You know, Doctor – Do – Little . . .Get it? Do Little.' There was only one player, I believe, who escaped a Prosser nickname. Anthony George Faulkner was already known as Charlie when he came to Pontypool. Pross never tried to change it or improve on it – apparently the explanation for it is a story in itself. All I can say is that it must have been a good one to have gagged Pross.

There's no doubt he saves the best of his wicked humour for our training sessions. It's all part of the psychology, of course, and very basic: 'You're running like the hairs on your arse are tied together' or 'Do these sit-ups properly and you'll have muscles on your guts like knots in a navvy's bootlace.' One of my personal Pross favourites was directed at a second XV player called in for first XV duty. Pross wanted to emphasise the youngster's failings as a line-out jumper. 'Jump' he bellowed, 'E.T., that extra-terrestial slug or whatever it is, can jump higher than you!'

Prosser's sayings are numerous. They are not always understood, and sometimes he is misquoted. 'Lions always go hunting on empty stomachs' was certainly one of his most famous sayings, but it was not the reason, as some believe, why the Pontypool Front Row ate little if anything from breakfast time to kick-off on the day of a match. I ate nothing because I believed eating before a match reduced my performance. Some also believed that because I had a certain order for preparing myself for a match, I was superstitious. It was nothing so romantic. I simply don't like rushing things. In the changing room I preferred everything to be in a logical order. It merely gave me peace of mind during the most tense moments before kick-off. It was more routine than ritual. What I do admit to, however, was preferring to run on to the field ahead of most of the players. I run on early not because of any superstitious quirk, but because I like to get the feel of the ball early. Some of the late arrivals don't get even a touch of the ball during the warm-up. And, in some circumstances, they might not touch it for a long time after that!

What most of us appreciate at Pontypool about Ray Prosser is that, unlike some, he does not hold an inquest immediately after a match. Every player knows when he has had a bad match, and although we know we may be in for a roasting, say, at the first training session of the next week, we all value not having post-mortems as we pull off our jerseys. Occasionally, Pross does the opposite, handing out praise and compliments when he knows players are down-in-the-mouth after a bad performance. It's all basic psychology, of course, as when after one match in which we had a lot of points scored against us, he ran into the changing room and laughingly shouted: 'Shut the doors quick, they'm coming through the windows'. Another different approach was after Pontypool had received a drubbing from Australia at Pontypool Park in 1981. No one was more disappointed than Ray Prosser on that occasion, but he did not show it at all. 'It's a game best forgotten' he said reassuringly, as we all sat glumly in our morgue-like changing room. He knew that every player was suffering his own personal mortification because the match had gone so badly, and he would never have dreamt of adding to our misery.

Later on, well after the match, the humiliation manifested itself in a variety of ways: Eddie Butler threatened to throw his boots into the nearby Afon Llwyd river, John Perkins sat in a corner, cried and then fell asleep; one of our supporters had a bout of fisticuffs with a town councillor outside the clubhouse; and Prosser told a bewildered Ray Williams, the WRU secretary, just what he thought of him. I delivered a short, carefully worded explanation of front-row technique to the referee, Roger Quittenton, and then got drunk.

If all this suggests there is never a dull moment when Ray

Prosser is at large, then that's the truth. The other side to him, Pross the slave-driver, the perfectionist, has been of benefit to all of us, players, our club and rugby in general. The game could do with more of his calibre and character.

My First Cap

Along with Charlie Faulkner, I won my first cap for Wales against France at Parc des Princes in Paris on 18 January 1975. It was just two months after my twenty-third birthday. Charlie, in contrast, was 34. We were the seventh and eighth props respectively that Wales had used since 1973, which may explain partly why they plumped finally for a comparative youngster and a veteran – disregarding the critics who suspected one of us was rather young and the other rather ancient (though, of course, no one knew Charlie's true age).

Charlie's immediate predecessors at loose-head were Glyn Shaw and Gerry Wallace. Mine were Walter Williams, Phil Llewellyn, Barrie Llewelyn and John Lloyd – the latter had played twice at tight-head even though he was normally a loose-head. This round-robin with the props was only part of the story for Wales were in the process of trying to rebuild their side after the modest performances of 1973–74 following the four previous glorious years.

Clearly, it was an opportune moment for all the new caps of 1975 – there were six, in total, against France – to prove themselves and to help give Wales a new identity. It was a challenge for all of us. At the same time no one was under any illusions. We had ample evidence of the selectors' policy: if you did not come up to their expectations, you were out.

I had special reason for caution, for I had been on the fringe of the Welsh team since 1972, and had been the victim of some curious selection decisions. My progress with Pontypool, for whom I had played since 1969, had been monitored by Ray Prosser. He insisted strongly that mastering the techniques of tight-head was as important as fitness, stamina and commitment. Even so, he must have been surprised when his protégé was called up for Trial duty in January 1972. If Ray was surprised, I was positively shocked when, after being selected as a reserve, I took the place of the legendary Denzil Williams, who had dropped out because of injury. At 20, my desire to add to Welsh schoolboy caps was strong, but, being realistic, the chance seemed a very long way off yet.

The more experienced players in the club could be easily categorised: forwards, particularly props, did not mature until their late twenties. Traditionally, the apprenticeship was long and hard; a few missing teeth, a scar or two and a cauliflower ear, were considered essential before you were accepted as a fully paid-up member of the Front Row Union.

That I was hardly qualified in any respect, did not diminish my enthusiasm for that Trial. If Wales wanted me, it was good enough. I was going to make the most of it. As ever, Pross prepared me for the biggest test of my life with words of advice: 'Don't' he ordered, 'Don't scrummage. Just save your energy for running about in the loose.' (Remember that scrummaging was not then the eight-man effort of today but was more a matter of personal choice: the hooker struck for the ball against the put-in; the tight-head either bent the loose-head or bored through, putting the opposing hooker at a disadvantage; and the loose-head tried to lift the tight-head. Often this resulted in a 'you leave me alone and I'll leave you alone', so that the props were able to be involved in the loose play.)

Naturally, I listened carefully to Prosser's advice. After all, who was I to question it? But, as a headstrong 20-year-old, I summed up the situation rather differently. I concluded that I was in the Trial to make up the numbers only and that I had no real chance of being picked for Wales. Therefore I decided that it would be much more useful to find out how I matched up to the other props in the Trial. I would scrummage in exactly the same way as I did for Pontypool. In those terms I was pleased with my performance, and on a few occasions I had put the opposition under pressure by scrummaging low. Once Jeff Young, Wales's very experienced hooker, told John Lloyd to allow the scrum to collapse so that they could reform and have a second bite of the cherry. At half-time, satisfaction gave way to bitter disappointment. I was taken off and replaced by Chris Charles.

As I took off my jersey I consoled myself that it had only been to give me experience and that I should not be unduly disappointed. I have since learned that the reason I was replaced was because the selectors considered I was taking such a hammering that I was likely to be injured. Apart from the fact that this was sheer nonsense, it showed that the selectors hadn't a clue when it came to scrummaging. Since when, for instance, does a loose-head take down a tight-head on his own put-in?

In any event, I returned to Pontypool to face Prosser. He asked me how I had got on and why they had taken me off at half-time. When I told him what I had done, and how well I thought I had scrummaged, he blew his top. 'I told you not to bloody scrummage', he roared, 'Didn't I say the idea was for you to save your energy and look impressive in the loose?' His argument soon became obvious. With four backs and a No. 8 on the selection panel, they would be looking only for what was done in the loose. The scrummaging did not matter on this occasion. Shamefacedly, I had to admit, Pross and not for the first time, was right.

Still it was a valuable early lesson. From that moment on I would treat selectors with caution, if not suspicion. However, it was encouraging to know that the Big Five considered I had something to offer. I was a late call-up for the first Trial at Swansea, 1972–73, when I played at loose-head, and was a reserve for both the final Trial and for Wales's tour of Canada.

Early in the 1973 season I played for East Wales against Australia at Newport. Once again I played as I did for Pontypool. I scrummaged low on our put-in. I lifted and drove on their put-in to place them under pressure. Imagine my surprise when Clive Rowlands, one of the selectors, came up to me in the changing room afterwards and declared: 'You've got to learn to hold and stay up'. It was all very confusing; Prosser was instructing me one way, and here I was being told I was doing it all wrong. Terry Cobner, who was sitting next to me, heard what Rowlands said. I asked him what he made of it and Cobner said, 'It had sounded like Rowlands thought you put too much into the scrummaging'. Terry was even more puzzled later in the season. He played in the Probables team in the final Trial, but the next day was considered not good enough to be included in the newly-announced squad. By the following Thursday, he was in the Wales team. Curious indeed are the ways of selectors.

My own progress up the ladder was by 1973–74 pretty well defined. After being called up to replace Walter Williams on the bench for Wales against Japan, it was off to Toulouse with Cobner, as captain, Bobby Windsor, Allan Martin and Geoff Wheel for Wales B against France B. I was off again at half-time, this time because of an ankle injury.

There were other lessons to be learned meanwhile. I played for East Wales against Tonga at the beginning of the next season, and I was not nearly fit enough. I suspect that none of the team were, which might explain why we lost. I was in much better shape, physically and mentally, for the next match, against New Zealand but while Faulkner and Windsor were picked to play, I was allocated my now usual place on the bench. A place in Wales's B victory over France at Cardiff and part of the Probables team which swamped the Possibles in the final Trial aroused speculation that, at last, I might be lucky. The line-up against France was to be announced to the press after the Trial, and John Dawes craftily suggested that Charlie and I go along to the Angel Hotel to listen to the announcement. Cliff Jones read out the team: 'J. P. R. Williams, T. G. R. Davies, S. P. Fenwick, R. W. R. Gravell, J. J. Williams, J. D. Bevan, G. O. Edwards, G. Price, R. W. Windsor, A. G. Faulkner, G. A. D. Wheel, A. J. Martin, T. P. Evans, T. J. Cobner, T. M. Davies' . . . . I can't remember very clearly now how I felt as I heard my name called out. My great moment had come, I was picked for Wales, and yet strangely I didn't feel elated or excited but just a sense of relief. I had made it!

The Pontypool Front Row

There are three Rs, three primary colours; there were three Furies, three Fates and three Graces. Alexander Dumas gave us *The Three Musketeers* and Max Boyce had his three forwards – the Pontypool Front Row.

As a Welsh speaker Max might have been tempted to call his rendering not a song but a triad, which in Welsh literature means a group of three stories. This is exactly what the Pontypool Front Row is, the story of three players from one club who, sometimes to their embarrassment, earned fame and repute throughout the rugby world. If for no other reason than I wore the No. 3 jersey, it is fitting that I take up where Max left off. Or at least try to fill in some of the gaps.

The Pontypool Front Row was born on 5 September 1973 when we first played together in Pontypool's colours against Pontypool District R.U. We became the first – and only – front-row unit from one club to play for Wales, against France in Paris on 18 January 1975. We were also the only club front row to play for the British Lions, which we did (yes, aptly enough) three times, the first being against Counties/Thames Valley at Pukekohe on 3 August 1977.

Give or take a few pounds, our vital statistics at our prime were: Bobby, 5 feet 9½ inches, 15 stone, 2 pounds; Charlie, 5 feet 10 inches, 15 stone 12 pounds; and myself 5 feet 10½ inches, 15 stone. I was born in 1951, which made me the youngest. Bobby was born in 1948 while Charlie arrived a little earlier, on one particular 27 February, making him the oldest.

Now, Charlie was always a little touchy about his age. When he was first chosen for Wales in 1975, his age varied between 27 and 30, depending on which newspaper you read or what figure our shrinking violet admitted to. In fact Charlie's age became the Great Guessing Game in Wales for quite a few seasons. One newspaper was so anxious to find out the truth that they assigned a reporter to search through the birth records of all Faulkners. The trouble was he was looking for a Charles Faulkner. No one had told him that Charlie was a nickname and that he should have been looking up Faulkner, Anthony George. Did the Welsh selectors know Charlie's real age, by the way? I can't be sure of that – except that they must have known at the end of the 1975 season because Charlie had to submit his passport to the WRU for the pre-tour formalities for the tour of the Far East. Years later, after all the fuss had died down, a reporter went up to Charlie at a rugby club bar. 'Come on, Charlie' he begged, 'how old are you, really?' Charlie (confirming that old habits die hard) thrust an empty pint glass towards the reporter and replied with a grin: 'Old enough, boy, old enough'.

The mystery about Charlie's age, and his sensitivity about it, is easily explained. The critics questioned the wisdom of Wales even considering picking someone as long in the tooth as Charlie, even though none of them knew how old he was. It wasn't a question of how good a prop Faulkner was, but in their wisdom whether those old legs of his would last the pace of an international. By accident or design, Charlie suddenly became 29, which the press agreed was not really that old. Young enough, in fact, to appease the critics and play for Wales. Three years later – by which time everyone thought he was 32 and therefore too old – there was something of a campaign to get him dropped in favour of a more 'mobile' prop. Those of us who knew the truth about Charlie's age found it difficult to conceal our amusement: Charlie was 34 when he was first capped. He was 38 when, after 19 appearances for Wales, injury ended his career. You could say, Charlie had the last laugh on everyone. He is still doing it. Now coach at Newport, he is not averse to turning out for them, if for some reason one of the regular front-row men can't play or is injured. But then, a coach does not have to produce his birth certificate. It's only a bit of paper, as Pross might say.

Although I was the junior member of the PFR, the other two had to doff their caps to me with regard to seniority at Pontypool. I had played, as a 17-year-old, for the second team in the 1968–69 season. I was still at school the following season when I made my first XV début. Although I played three first XV matches that season only, I regularly trained with the club. I was keen enough, as it happened, to prefer to wander around Pontypool for up to two hours after school, waiting for training to start, rather than going straight home by bus to Glascoed and then returning by bus to begin training.

I was therefore fairly well established at Pontypool when Charlie joined the club from Cross Keys for the 1972–73 season. Until then I had alternated between loose- and tight-head, though I preferred loose-head, the position in which I had won my schoolboy caps and had played for Monmouthshire. The arrival of Charlie, an out-and-out loose-head, determined my position. From then on, I was to play tight-head. It was to prove the making of both of us, though of course neither of us realised it at the time. Charlie's arrival was important in another respect. He gave stability and power to the front row, which I am convinced was a major factor in Pontypool becoming Welsh club champions that season. We had begun clawing our way up from being the worst team in Wales the previous season, when Terry Cobner's captaincy and Ray Prosser's coaching were at last beginning to bear fruit.

Charlie joined us at an opportune time but he was by no means the finished product. Although he was immensely strong and rugged, his technique was, to say the least, crude and unrefined. Under Pross's inspiring direction, however, he emerged as the most respected scrummaging loose-head in Wales. Since the basis of Pontypool's forward play was to wear down the opposition in the scrums, this made Charlie's contribution all the more significant. At his peak, I have no hesitation in saying that Faulkner was the most ruthless loose-head scrummager I ever played with or against.

The trinity was completed in the 1973–74 season when Windsor, who had previously played with Cardiff and Cross

Keys, and had been long-established as Wales's reserve hooker, came to Pontypool Park. It was taken for granted that Bobby would succeed Jeff Young in the Wales side, for Jeff was on the point of retiring anyway. Bobby won his first cap, against Australia, on 10 November 1973 as a fledgling Pontypool player. In fact, Bobby had already played for Pontypool at the end of the previous season, against Newbridge, at tight-head because I was injured. There were problems over Bobby's transfer from Cross Keys; but the important point was that he had joined. Thus the Pontypool Front Row was formed.

The Viet Gwent had arrived and a legend was born. It is interesting, now, to find out how others saw us. Clem Thomas and Geoffrey Nicholson in *Welsh Rugby: The Crowning Years* (Collins) wrote: 'To the Welsh public they were like the three musketeers, intensely loyal to each other, to Pontypool and to Wales – and probably in that order. When occasionally Charlie for any reason was out of the side they grieved with him and then consoled him and each other, and whenever he re-emerged, as when he flew out as a replacement for the Lions in 1977, the other two were as overjoyed as puppies who had found a lost member of their litter.'

Others might balk at the image of us as puppies. Bulldogs perhaps. Or Dobermans. Harsh words have been said and written about our uncompromising attitude and approach. My reply is that each member of the PFR can hardly put his hand on his heart and claim 'I'm innocent'. Each one of us, different in temperament, interests and background, learned pretty quickly that to survive in big-time rugby, we had to develop mental as well as physical hardness. Possibly the other two, being ex-steelworkers, had the edge on me in this respect. Charlie, a black belt at judo, knew a little more than either Bobby or me about close-quarter combat! It goes without saying, that this meant we were reasonably well prepared to handle most situations; and when one of us was getting a bit of a going-over, the other two immediately went to his assistance.

This co-operation was based on our innate survival policy,

rather than out of loyalty or friendship. We each did our jobs on the field; at the same time it was part of a team effort. There was a distinct advantage, of course, in being a unit. Each of us knew the other's strong points and was aware of each other's problems in certain situations. We coped because we knew we had to. Adaptability became our key word, and that stemmed from our recognition and understanding of each other's job. Our approach plus the fact that we seemed to blend together perfectly, helped create an aura of invincibility about the Pontypool Front Row. We felt we were just doing our jobs: it was our opponents, or those that watched us play, who created the legend. None of us, including Bobby, who also had to hook the ball, ever lost sight of the fact that, in essence, our job on the field was to scrummage – and scrummage damned hard. Our job was physical and tough. You beat them, or they beat you. A punch, a raking, a boot in the head – occasionally anything goes in the front row. I'm not defending it. But then let's face it, we are involved in the most fiercely competitive area on the rugby field and the demands on strength, stamina and commitment are high. Pride is also important. A prop does not have to be a thug or on a short fuse (very, very few of them are). But if he is getting stuffed by his opponent, he can either do nothing or he can react violently but there usually isn't enough time for this before he is needed in the next scrum, maul, or ruck.

It follows that front-row men have no illusions: they have to be realists. Quite simply, if one of us got the better of his opposite number, he had done well. He had done his job. If all three of us did, our team, whether it was Pontypool, Monmouthshire, Wales or the Lions, were halfway to winning. Such are the tenets of front-row play, as they have always been and I hope always will be.

Understandably, I suppose, everyone thought of the members of the PFR as great friends, whose common interest on the rugby field extended to their private lives. This was not strictly true. Each of us had different outside interests and involvements, and it was rare that we got together socially. I would say mutual respect governed our relationship; it was camaraderie

LEFT Nice legs, pity about the dress. Yours truly, aged two, at home in Blackpool in 1952.

BELOW Getting acclimatised at Pontypool Park in 1970, aged 18.

ABOVE LEFT Bobby Windsor, going for a loose ball for Wales against Australia, at Cardiff Arms Park on 20 December 1975. ABOVE RIGHT Ray Prosser, the greatest coach of forwards in the world. *South Wales Argus*

ABOVE Charlie Faulkner, who was deceptively quick for a loose-head prop, tears through to score a try in Wales' 32–11 victory against Ireland at Cardiff Arms Park in 1975. *Colorsport*

ABOVE The Pontypool Front Row getting ready to scrum down for the British Lions against Bay of Plenty at Rotorua on 9 August 1977. The PFR played together three times on the tour. *Colorsport*

RIGHT Fran Cotton, the anchor man of England's front row 1971–81, who made many notable contributions to the British Lions in South Africa and New Zealand. *Associated Sports Photography*

ABOVE Ian 'Mighty Mouse' McLauchlan, of Scotland, who was technically the best loose-head prop I faced in my career. *Colorsport*

ABOVE An old adversary. France's Gerard 'Garth' Cholley, who notwithstanding his uncouth approach, was one of the strongest props in international rugby. *Colorsport*

LEFT Just to prove that rugby players do spend some time at home . . . with daughters Joanne and Louise on the flanks and the latest Price arrival, Owen, trying on one of my caps for size.

BELOW My daughter Joanne curiously examines my eye injury suffered during the Wales-France match at Cardiff Arms Park on 6 March 1976.

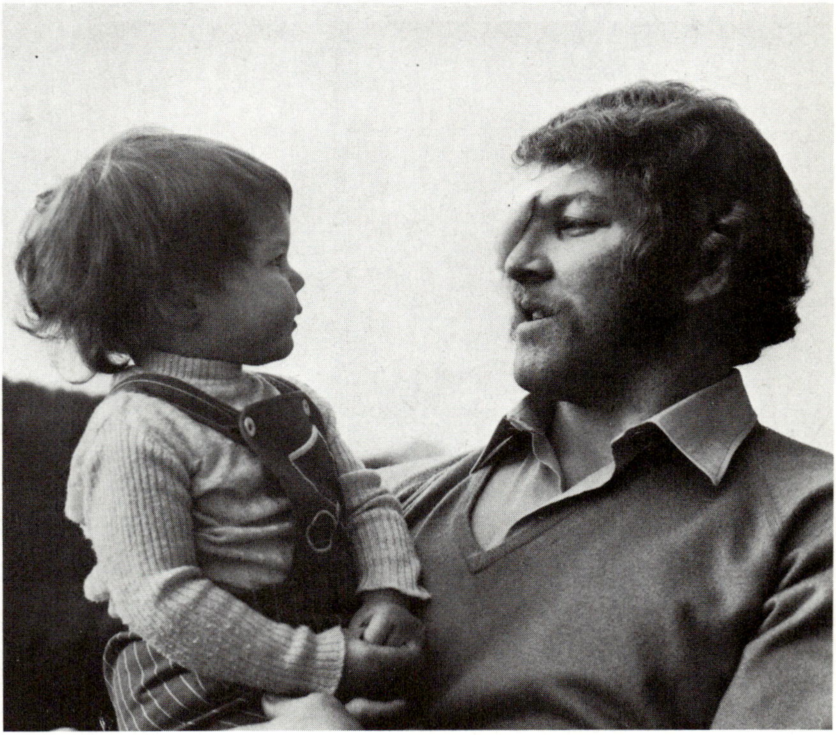

ABOVE Robert Paparemborde, the French tight-head prop. 'Papa's' unorthodox technique and unusual physique made him the scourge of loose-head props. *Associated Sports Photography*

ABOVE Sometimes you can only stand and stare. Despite some transgression, appealed for by John Robbie (*right*), Louis Moolman feeds the ball out to Tony du Plessis in the Northern Transvaal-Lions match at Loftus, Pretoria in 1980. *Bob Thomas*

ABOVE LEFT Cultural exchange during the British Lions' tour of South Africa in 1980. *The Star.* ABOVE RIGHT Getting in some line-out practice against Natal at King's Park, Durban, on 17 May 1980 when the British Lions won 21–15. *Bob Thomas*

ABOVE A jubilant Peter Wheeler and John Robbie (*right*) and Allan Martin (*left*) in the Lions' changing room after we had beaten the Springboks 17–13 in the Fourth Test at Loftus Versfeld, Pretoria, on 12 July 1980. *Colorsport*

ABOVE One of my two tries on the 1980 Lions' tour of South Africa against Transvaal at Johannesburg on 7 June.

ABOVE Leaving Sydney Cricket Ground on 17 June 1978 with a broken jaw, courtesy of Steve Finanne. *Colorsport*

rather than true friendship. This is not to say that we did not often enjoy each other's company. The common bond of being members of the Front Row Union guarantees get-togethers off the field. But there were times when a glance or a cutting remark revealed the other side to our relationship.

In 1974 the British Lions toured South Africa and Tonga came to Britain in the early part of the new season. The Tongans won one match only out of ten, their first, beating an East Wales side in which Charlie and myself played. I was in the side only because Mike Knill, the Cardiff policeman, was unfit. Enough to say, neither Charlie nor I had a particularly good match. Everyone's thoughts, however, were on other visitors, New Zealand, who were following behind the Tongans with a short tour of Ireland, Wales and England. Wales, though having decided that the match with the All Blacks was an unofficial international – incredibly we played the old enemy as a Welsh XV with no caps awarded – left few stones unturned when they selected their squad. They called up no fewer than six props, including Colin Smart, the Englishman playing for Newport. Smart politely turned down the Welsh invitation.

Bobby and Charlie, however, were picked to play against New Zealand. Barrie Llewelyn, of Llanelli, went in on the tight-head and I found myself on the subs' bench. As the match took place on 27 November, Wales still had time to stage a Trial before the first Championship match, against France in January. Clearly, there was still hope for me to join Bobby and Charlie. As it turned out, we not only played together in the Trial, but we were all picked to play against France. The Pontypool Front Row was now the Wales Front Row. It was Bobby's sixth appearance for Wales, but it was Charlie's and my first. I thought the PFR did well in Paris, a match we won 25–10. Bobby may have had some reservations: Albert Estève's punches in the scrums from the second row were hardly intended to improve his looks. Eventually, Bobby decided enough was enough, and when he got the opportunity, he booted Estève in the mouth. Albert's only response was a smile and a wink. I don't think I'll ever understand French players!

The rest of that 1975 season proved the selectors were right about the PFR. Wales lost only to Scotland, beat Ireland by a record 32–4 and ended up winning the Championship. While, of course, we were in our element having achieved our ambitions of playing for Wales, we were only just beginning to realise that we had embarked on full-time rugby careers. There were to be no more seasons, no more breaks. Winter and summer overlapped for no sooner had the 1975 Championship finished than off we went, with Wales, to Hong Kong and Japan. On our return, there was more preparation for another touring party, this time the Australians.

If the players showed signs of wear and tear, it was hardly surprising. The PFR proved to be no exception – all three of us had to pass fitness tests on the Thursday before the first Championship match of 1976, against England at Twickenham. Charlie had a shoulder injury, Bobby had a rib injury and I had torn knee ligaments. Charlie shrugged off his problem easily enough. Bobby and I had to be a little more cunning. Bobby was in a great deal of pain, but he came out of an examination with the Welsh medical officer, Gordon Rowley, with a smile of relief on his face. He had been passed fit because Gordon had examined the side of Bobby's rib cage which was perfectly healthy. I don't know how Bobby could have forgotten to tell the Doc on which side the injury was!

I followed Bobby into the examination room. Gordon bent my knee, twisted it this way and that, compared its size with the other knee, prodded my ligaments, and after much humming and hawing he asked me if I was in any pain. I said no, trying to put on my most innocent look. Gordon then asked me if I thought I would be fit enough to play in my present condition. Lying through my teeth I said of course I would. I suppose all doctors are sceptical and Gordon sent me out on to the field for a series of exercises supervised by Gerry Lewis, the Welsh team physiotherapist. Luckily, Gerry gave me all the exercises that I was able to do. I'd have been in trouble had he asked me, for instance, to change direction when running. Of course, I'd taken a risk in protesting my fitness, reasoning that I still had a couple of days in which to get 100 per cent. We all came through the match at Twickenham – where Wales won impressively 21–9 – and afterwards Dr Rowley asked me how the knee was. I told him that it was aching a bit to which he replied: 'I'll tell you the story about that knee some other time'. I knew then that he knew I shouldn't have played. You can fool only some of the people some of the time . . .

Despite the fact that Wales were having tremendous success since the PFR had been called to duty, an 'anti-Faulkner' campaign had started for the 1977 Championship. Wales wanted a younger, more mobile prop, they said. Consequently Charlie found himself dropped for the first two matches, but his scrummaging ability was so badly missed that he was recalled to play against England at Cardiff. Charlie, unfortunately, had to drop out through injury, which gave Clive Williams, of Swansea, his chance. Clive, a very good loose-head technically, made the most of the opportunity and was retained for the last match, against Scotland. The break-up of the Pontypool Front Row seemed complete when Clive was selected as one of the two British Lions loose-head props for the tour of 1977. Charlie was left behind, on stand-by duty. That may well have been that, had not Clive been injured in New Zealand – and Charlie was flown out to replace him. Several loose-heads had been short-listed by the Four Home Unions, but the front-row men in New Zealand could vote for who they wanted: Charlie was their man, they declared unanimously.

Charlie, of course, was unaware of all this. He was back in Wales, in fact, attending a WRU coaching course run by Ray Williams at Aberystwyth. When the news of Clive's injury came through, Ray realised that Charlie might be called up. Shrewdly Ray also told John Lawrence, secretary of the Four Home Unions tours committee, that Charlie was 'fit and available'. Lawrence said he would have to check on other players before making a decision. Everyone at Aberystwyth was thus on tenterhooks for nearly a week while Lawrence went through his short list. If it was a fit Faulkner they wanted, then a fit Faulkner they'd get, decided Ray. Accordingly Charlie was put to work on his fitness and running by Ray, something not usually demanded of would-be coaches at Aberystwyth. And whenever Charlie seemed to show signs of slacking during his running, Ray shouted: 'Come on, Charlie, remember New Zealand'. On the last day of the course, a Friday, Charlie was still hard at work in one of three open-air sessions. 'I'll never forget it,' said Ray Williams, 'Suddenly there was this figure running towards us, shouting and waving.' The figure was the registrar of the Aberystwyth Agricultural College, who had answered a call from John Lawrence. Charlie was in! After listening to the message from the out-of-breath registrar, Ray at once blew his whistle to stop the sessions. 'Charlie,' Ray shouted, 'pack your bags, you're on your way.' Everyone cheered as Charlie came running up. 'I won't let you down' he blurted out, 'I won't let you down.'

It took Charlie 30 hours to get to New Zealand. He arrived in time to take part in one of the most strenuous scrummaging sessions we had on that tour. He was still a little jet-lagged when he joined us on the flight from Auckland to Dunedin. 'What's this place Dundee like' he inquired innocently. We had only just stopped laughing at that when someone asked him: 'Which way did you travel out here? Through Los Angeles?' Charlie pondered for a moment. 'No' he said. 'L.A.!' There were only three weeks of the tour left when Charlie joined it. He fitted in as if he had been with us from the beginning. He was undoubtedly a great tourist.

Charlie was most fastidious about his appearance on the field and particularly about his shorts. He positively hated baggy shorts, which seemed to emphasise his gawky, thin legs. He was none too pleased either, when I nicknamed him 'sparrow legs', responding with remarks about my beer pot. Bobby said that I played better with the beer pot than I did without! On a tour, particularly a long one, the comic and joker has a very important role. Bobby assumed it in New Zealand in 1977 and he made a marvellous contribution to team morale. Sometimes he was spectacularly successful. On one occasion, at the Avon

Park Motel in Christchurch, he decided to use the fire hose to get one of the players out of bed. Unfortunately, Bobby chose the wrong room. One of the ordinary hotel guests had a rather nasty shock! Bobby seemed to like playing a fireman. At a particularly grotty hotel in Whangarei, the team were consoling themselves with a few beers and a sing-song at 2 a.m. It was not, incidentally, a spontaneous party. Everyone was summoned to attend whether they wanted to go or not: Moss Keane invited me, after breaking down the door of my room and dragging me out of bed by the ankles. In the circumstances, it was not surprising that the boys raised little objection when Bobby decided to light a small fire in the middle of the room where the party was held, using beer cartons, beer mats and any other item at hand, including a rather dilapidated easy chair. Suddenly Bobby raced from the room and returned almost immediately with the fire hose full on and shouting 'Fire! Fire!' Quite a few of us were drenched as our hero stopped his little blaze from getting out of control.

On the playing side of the tour, Bobby was extremely unlucky to have been dropped after the first Test at Wellington. We had lost, but the only area where we matched the All Blacks up front was in the scrummage. Phil Orr was at loose-head and I was at tight-head, and we pushed them about quite a bit. For that alone, Bobby deserved to be included in the second Test. Peter Wheeler gave a storming display in our next match, against a combined side at Timaru (incidentally the match in which Bill Beaumont made his first Lions appearance), and he took Bobby's place at Christchurch. Once in the Test side, Wheeler was difficult to dislodge. He was a very good hooker, but certainly not better, at the time, than Bobby. As is often the case, however, one player had to be unlucky.

Ray Prosser considers Bobby to be the finest all-round hooker he has seen. No player could receive higher praise. Bobby's greatest asset was his strength. He was the strongest scrummaging hooker I ever knew; adaptable enough to be able to switch to loose-head (which he did many times for Pontypool) or to tight-head, a position he played in for the Lions against Waikato in our eighteenth match in New Zealand. I wonder what Jim Telfer, the 'I'll do it my way' 1983 Lions coach, would have made of him, for Bobby always liked to get involved in the running of the Lions' coaching sessions. A session rarely went by without some contribution from Bobby; similarly he always had something constructive to say on the field. He even advised referees on occasions! Bobby knew everything there was to know about scrummaging and front-row play, and if sometimes he appeared flippant, it merely disguised an innate and thorough knowledge which very few players possessed. His game did not begin and end in the front row. He was, for instance, expert at initiating the rolling maul. He recognised he was in the ideal position to do this, for as a hooker he was the last man up from the tight scrum, which meant he was among the last to the breakdown, from where he could direct second phase operations. Some players simply arrive at a breakdown and either flop on top of it or fringe, waiting for someone else to create something. Bobby was never like that. He was a natural, born leader of forwards.

He was desperately unlucky not to have become Wales's most-capped hooker. He made 27 successive appearances for Wales and probably would have beaten Bryn Meredith's 34-cap record, but for an extraordinary incident which ruled him out against England in the final Championship match of 1979. He had played for Pontypool against Cardiff in a Cup match shortly before, and ended up in hospital with severe lime burns on his back because the field had been marked out with the wrong material. Why he was the only player to be hurt, we'll never know. But it kept him out of the Welsh team, giving Alan Phillips, of Cardiff, his chance. Bobby came back to play against Romania on 6 October 1979, but Phillips had by now won many admirers and it was he, rather than Bobby, who was chosen to hook for Wales in the 1980 campaign. Bobby was not fit enough because of a back injury to be considered before the 1980 international season. A totally fit Windsor, I'm sure, would have been Wales's No. 1 choice, but by now anyway he was in acute pain. It was diagnosed as a slipped disc and after a laminectomy which is the removal of the disc by surgery – an operation which has ended many players' careers – it was clear he would never play international rugby again. Many players would have settled for that; but not Bobby. Amazingly, he not only fought his way back to fitness, but he started playing again as captain of Pontypool's second team. On numerous occasions, he even turned out for the first XV, not only as hooker but sometimes at loose-head prop, and frequently as captain. You just can't keep Bobby down.

Ironically, Faulkner's international career ended at precisely the same time as Bobby's. He damaged a knee in the same match against Cardiff in which Bobby was burned, so he too missed the England match. His injury was much more severe, however, for he had to have an operation to remove a cartilage. Two days after the operation I visited Charlie at the Heath Hospital in Cardiff. 'When are you going to be allowed home?', I inquired. 'In about a week,' replied Charlie. 'The doctor has told me I've got to be able to do a particular exercise with my leg before they let me out, and it's normally about a week after the operation before the exercise can be done.' I asked: 'What exercise is it then, Charlie?' I should have known better. 'It's like this' he said, not only explaining the exercise but lifting his leg up and down several times in the required manner!

So the Pontypool Front Row's last appearance for Wales was on 17 February 1979, against France, at Parc des Princes, coincidentally the same venue where we had made our début. We would have liked to have gone out on the same high note as we had entered the international game. But France won 14–13, largely thanks to a fine try by Gourdon. In all the PFR played 20 times for Wales over five years. In that period Wales won the Championship each year, and the Grand Slam twice. We could have been forgiven if we began to think we were unbeatable for the run of success included 11 victories on the trot, and four of our five defeats were by two and one point margins. And our only defeat on Welsh soil was courtesy of Roger Quittenton, that controversial match, 12–13 against the All Blacks.

The Pontypool Front Row's full record for Wales was:

1975　W 25–10 France
　　　 W 20–4　England
　　　 L 10–12 Scotland
　　　 W 32–4　Ireland　　　　　Championship winners

1976　W 28–3　Australia
　　　 W 21–9　England
　　　 W 28–6　Scotland
　　　 W 34–9　Ireland
　　　 W 19–13　France　　　　　Grand Slam winners
　　　 W 20–19 Argentina

1978　W　9–6　England
　　　 W 22–14 Scotland
　　　 W 20–16 Ireland
　　　 W 16–7　France　　　　　Grand Slam winners
　　　 L　8–18 Australia
　　　 L 17–19 Australia
　　　 L 12–13 New Zealand

1979　W 19–13 Scotland
　　　 W 24–21 Ireland
　　　 L 13–14 France　　　　　Championship winners

Charlie, incidentally, played his last match for Pontypool against Oxford on 25 October 1980. It was also the last (serious) occasion when the Pontypool Front Row played together. Bobby, as I've said, is still very active at Pontypool, while Anthony George Faulkner has become an influential coach at Newport. I've got some good colleagues in the front row at Pontypool in the Jones boys, Steve and Staff. It's not quite the same, of course, and never could be. It was unique that one club should have produced an all-international front row. The PFR was quite exceptional and each of us is very proud that we belonged to it.

The Pontypool Way

Pontypool has not exactly been the most popular of rugby clubs over the past few years. Our critics have not been slow in coming forward. We are accused of playing either a boring, yawn-inducing game or behaving like animals on the field. Praise is about as rare as a visit from Halley's comet. No doubt envy plays a part. A club which wins consistently, as we have done in recent years, and which regularly produces quality players who deprive others of a chance of representative rugby, will understandably cause some resentment.

However, I believe our unsavoury reputation stems as much from the way we play, let us call it our tactical approach, as it does from incidents during matches. In simple terms, our chief tactic is to deprive the opposition of the ball and maintain that possession among our forwards, where traditionally our team strength lies. To the casual observer, who enjoys watching the pendulum of attack and counterattack of two evenly-matched sides, I must admit it must be a bit boring at times. While, as a player, I see no reason to defend our approach, it must be appreciated that the Pontypool Way is not the result of a set, rigid policy, but has evolved out of necessity. The turning point is often difficult to identify but I suppose you must look back to the 1970–71 season when the campaign to establish Pontypool as a top club began. Up to then, we were probably the worst team in Wales, losing more often than we won, despondent, dejected and resigned to our fate. The problem was that we had few players of outstanding skill. So we decided to compromise: to make do with effort and commitment, allied to sensible tactical play. Gradually, our fortunes changed. We began to win, and when we did lose usually it was only by the odd point or two. After all the previous setbacks and time wasted preparing for defeat, this was a remarkable turnabout. Suddenly there was a smile on the face of the tiger, as well as on Ray Prosser's who was instrumental in our change of tactics.

Having found the formula, and as the saying goes success breeds success, we reckoned that at last we were on the right path. We stuck rigidly to the formula for that reason, even though some considered our style unattractive and therefore we became unpopular. All I can say is that though we did not have many friends, we had self-respect.

The development has continued. Today Pontypool play a positive 15-man game and either we have to perform pretty badly or our opposition have to excel for us to lose. There can be no better example of this than our record in the Welsh Cup over the last three years – we have been beaten only once, and that was inconclusively, by Newbridge.

Unfortunately, like habits, reputations also die hard. Where did it all start? It is impossible to answer. I can speak from personal experience only. Possibly the starting point of our 'bad boys' image was in 1973–74 when, as Welsh champions, we travelled up to play London Welsh, champions of the previous season and Britain's outstanding club side of the late 1960s and early 1970s. There was no way we were going to try to match them at their fluent, running game. We played it our way: a hard scrummaging, rucking, driving, tight game. I didn't think it went down too well with the crowd, who had been used to seeing their side overwhelm the opposition by running rugby, a style which was well suited to the players they had at the time.

In the event, several of their players were injured. I remember the 'incidents' clearly. Their full-back was rucked over and suffered a head injury; a centre went off after a tackle with an old rib injury; and with the crowd now less than amused by this time, they went wild when their fly-half and flanker had to be treated for head injuries even though they had collided when attempting to tackle one of our players. The atmosphere was hostile when in the closing minutes, the only incident which might be termed dirty, occurred. The victim was Clive Rees, who was high tackled when he tried to cut back inside.

The ill-feeling among spectators influenced the London Welsh committee, and as a result fixtures between the clubs were abandoned. It was a sad, regrettable day for both clubs. Nothing occurred in that match to warrant relations being severed. It makes you wonder how many now regret their hasty, ill-considered comments at the time. In my opinion, for instance, John Taylor over-reacted and aired his views rather too loudly. John Dawes, too, was quoted as saying: 'our players are not accustomed to this type of game'. My view is that London Welsh were not used to losing so heavily and to being dominated and restricted by another team at home. It is significant that the referee (who was, I believe, a London Society official) did not admonish any of our players for any kind of foul play. I received, by the way, a black eye in the match, courtesy of a punch from a British Lions lock forward. We didn't complain about that. As a postscript: I understand efforts are being made to restore good relations between the clubs and that there are hopes, on both sides, of annual fixtures being resumed. Personally I think this will be a good thing, for both London Welsh and Pontypool.

Anyhow, 'give a dog a bad name', Pontypool had suddenly acquired a reputation and we were stuck with it. Even after the most mundane fracas or mild flare-up, Pontypool were blamed every time. The next match where the mud was thrown and then stuck, was against Swansea in March 1977. This so-called notorious, dirty match resulted in a 17–15 win to Pontypool and as the score suggests, it was a close and entertaining contest. You do not have to take my word for that. Dewi Bebb, one of the more perceptive of Welsh critics, felt compelled to come into the Pontypool changing room afterwards and congratulate the players for their part in one of the most attractive and exciting matches he had watched that season. His words, not mine. The atmosphere too in our clubhouse was warm and friendly, with their players drinking the champagne that was opened to celebrate the selection of some of their players and ours for the Lions tour of New Zealand. There was not the slightest indication that Swansea were about to break off fixtures.

The bombshell fell the following Monday when the *Western Mail* published accusations by three of the Swansea players, complaining of being punched, among other things. Not a word was said about one of our players who was sent home suffering from concussion. We didn't complain about that. Swansea, at that time, were hardly restrained when it came to the rough stuff; in the light of unsavoury incidents concerning them in recent years, nothing has been done to improve their image either. 'Let he who hath no sin cast the first stone . . .'

It has also been supposed that the reason Pontypool do not play Llanelli on a regular basis is because of dirty play in the past. The facts are much less controversial. The problem with the fixtures arose at committee level; they failed to confirm our traditional date, after a few promptings from us. Consequently Pontypool arranged to play Cardiff instead on that date, which apparently offended Llanelli so much that thereafter they would not renew fixtures. There is a saying that you cannot find a more small-minded person than a club committee man. I'm beginning to believe it.

On the playing front, it seems, every incident in which Pontypool are involved attracts attention because of our reputation. We have no angels at Pontypool, but there again, nor has any other club. Ten of our forwards have been picked to represent Wales and seven of those have toured with the Lions. This is indisputable evidence that selectors want what we've got to offer. The top referees, too, admit that they never have trouble refereeing us, and many say we play fairly. Yet if a Pontypool player is sent off, it somehow seems worse because he is a Pontypool player; we are inevitably held responsible for any difference of opinion, no matter how expressed, that takes place on the field.

At Pontypool, we don't complain when we are on the receiving end. As John Perkins says, for every stitch inserted in opposing players, we have had two ourselves. We didn't complain when Perky was kicked in the mouth by the Ebbw

Vale centre, Alan Tovey, who must have run 25 yards to practise his dental skill in a ruck (Tovey, incidentally, was made out to be something of a hero, when in the *Western Mail*, he announced his retirement because of the rough standards in the game. If I remember correctly there was also something about a message from God.) Ron Floyd didn't complain, either, after he was kicked in the face while standing in a line-out during our match against the French champions, Agen, in 1974. Floyd was 6 feet 5 inches, so some acrobatics were required for that damage to be inflicted. After that match, Prosser invited Mike Boon (*Sunday Express*) into our changing room to show him the stud-marks on my back which I had received, also standing up, at the kick-off. 'Take a good look, Mike', said Pross, 'that's the sort of thing we receive but do not complain about.' Nothing was said, either, after a Cardiff lock forward, notorious for his brand of pugilism, took a fancy to punching me in the head when I was down in a scrum.

I realise that all this might sound a little defensive, but the truth is that all clubs have their deliberately dirty players, all have players who are on a short fuse, and all possess players who start trouble to disguise their shortcomings and lack of ability. What I would like to know is why Pontypool are picked on more than these other clubs. Our reputation seems to be irredeemable. I remember one season when we had no players sent off, but wherever we went we were still called animals.

In fact, whenever we play at St Helen's the Swansea crowd take up the chant: 'Animals, animals, animals'. I'm convinced that this started back in 1976, after we had played Swansea in the Welsh Cup semi-final on Sunday, 28 March. It was the match in which Mervyn Davies collapsed and nearly died after suffering a brain haemorrhage. By Monday morning, rumours were rife that Mervyn had been the victim of some Pontypool misdemeanour. While Mervyn was fighting for his life, Pontypool were being slated. Fortunately, on Monday night, television highlights revealed the truth: Mervyn collapsed while running in open play, with no other player near him. Certainly his collapse was not the result of any contact with a

Pontypool player. We felt relieved that we had been exonerated. The surgeon who tended Mervyn also confirmed that the damage could have been caused at any time during his career. We were disappointed, however, when Mervyn took so long after his complete recovery, to dispel publicly any doubts that Pontypool were in any way to blame – and it was only after he was prompted to do so by Bobby Windsor.

Yet despite this, the following season Pontypool ran on to St Helen's to a hostile reception. I can assume only that the Swansea supporters blamed us for the Mervyn Davies incident, regardless of the truth. We were held responsible for an illness that could have struck him down anywhere – driving his car or shopping with his wife. In fact, he was lucky that it happened in a match where doctors were in attendance. Their swift diagnosis and his immediate admittance to hospital probably saved his life.

We fell foul of a WRU reprimand following our club tour to the USA in 1979. We were banned from touring overseas for three years because of the trouble on that tour. Aside from the rights or wrongs of the tour and our punishment, I think it is important to say that much of the problem stemmed from the fact that the American players and officials were not ready for our type of rugby. I think it was a frustrating experience for them because, as an emergent rugby nation, they were looking for what could be described as the finer points of the game, the running and the handling. The physical, purposeful, forward type of game caught them unprepared, and they reacted against it. I don't suppose that the WRU took that into account. They banned us because of the incidents on the tour, the sending off of Steve Sutton and John Perkins, and Jeff Squire taking off the whole team during the last match, against BATS in San Francisco.

The four-match tour had got off to a good start. In the first match at San Diego, the referee was a New Zealander who allowed us to use the traditional form of rucking, but that the local players disliked. An American refereed our second match, against Pacific Coast in Los Angeles. He certainly did not appreciate our style of forward play. As it turned out, this did not make any difference. We were beaten by the heat – 94°F – and by the speed and skill of their backs.

The real trouble started in the third match, against a San Francisco President's XV. Whether our reputation had preceded us, I have no way of knowing. But their pack contained players with a reputation for being hard men, or so we were told. Not surprisingly, it was a bit of a rough contest. Perkins had an early bath.

Our last match, against BATS, was a travesty of refereeing. The referee Dennis Shanahar, was an Irish-American, who was clearly determined to favour the home side with blatantly incorrect decisions. Sutton received his marching orders early on, but Shanahar's obvious bias was really needling us. The final straw was when he allowed the BATS scrum-half to pick the ball out of our scrum, while it was still under Jeff's feet. I don't think anyone has seen such flagrant disregard of the Laws go unpunished. 'That's it boys, let's get out of here', Jeff announced, and we all followed him off the field just before half-time.

At the time everyone was so incensed with the referee, that no one, including our tour manager, Tony Simons, questioned whether Jeff had done the right thing. Later, I suppose, when we had calmed down, most of us regretted the decision and considered that perhaps Jeff had been a little hasty. It is worth recording, though, that at the previous match Shanahar had been marching around the pitch, bringing to the crowd's attention certain things Pontypool were doing on the field and threatening: 'I'll put a stop to these on Friday'. Shanahar did not realise it, but Tony Simons heard him. I mention it here, only to add a biographical note on one of the most controversial referees I've come across.

The following year, Bath undertook a similar tour of the United States and also ran foul of Shanahar. Subsequently, the Bath fixture secretary, John Roberts, wrote a personal letter to Rod Morgan, chairman of the Welsh selectors, expressing his sympathy at what had happened to Pontypool at the hands of the referee. I understand John Roberts even suggested we might have been victimised. England too in 1982 had cause for complaint, in their match handled by Shanahar in Dallas. Pontypool, incidentally, are not the only team to have 'done a run job' in that part of the United States. Ponsonby, of New Zealand, also trooped off during a match in 1980. I have no idea who the referee was on that occasion . . . but I wouldn't be surprised if it was someone with an aversion for the Union Jack!

One last thought on Pontypool's approach to the game. The most important thing to realise in rugby football is that when all the dust has settled, the excitement and the post-mortems over, it's only the winners who are remembered. The most important statistic in the record book is the result. Results decide championships and competitions, while entertainment is secondary. From a player's point of view, the most important consideration is his reputation – whether it has been damaged or enhanced. Coaches too have their priorities as they base their success first on winning, then on attractiveness of play. A side which has played attractive rugby, and lost, will receive a certain amount of credit for the way they played. But the side will be quickly dismissed, regardless of the way they play, if they lose consistently.

Selectors are loathe to change a winning team. Therefore, from a personal point of view, players are happier winning because it means they have a better chance of keeping their place in the side. Winning helps breed confidence which leads to a higher standard of play. The whole principle of selecting a representative side is based on winning. Selectors do not watch clubs like Penarth or sides which lose consistently. They watch sides that win regularly, which implies that players of a successful club are of a higher standard.

I believe it is better to win, than to feel second-rate. Attractiveness, in a rugby sense, is relative. The casual observer prefers to see the ball thrown about, rather than a tight match. The more informed observer appreciates the finer points of back play and the involvement of forwards in loose play. But it takes a connoisseur to appreciate a skilful forward battle.

I find a match in which the ball is thrown about just for the sake of it as boring as an unskilful forward battle. I much prefer to watch a tactical battle between two sides of completely contrasting styles: for instance, a team which has a powerful pack of forwards whose aim is to overwhelm by dominating possession and using the forwards to run at the opposition in loose play, rolling mauls, inter-passing and so on, playing against a side which is more skilled behind and which realises that they can win only by running and handling with every crumb of possession they can wring out.

Enjoyment comes from success – that is the realising of ambitions. At top level, internationals, the satisfaction comes from having been there and having done it, rather than enjoying the game. Matches are too hard and the pressure too great for it to be otherwise.

The Barbarians

The Barbarian Football Club, or as they are better known, the Baa-baas, were founded in 1890. They are a club without a ground, charge no subscriptions and are supposed to have no funds. They have a reputation for playing open, attractive rugby. It is also believed that players regard it as an honour to play for them, the next best thing to being picked for one's country.

I know of at least three players who would decline that honour – Charlie Faulkner, Bobby Windsor and myself. I don't suppose many players have told our famous Baa-baas to get stuffed but we have, and with good cause. The trouble, and the rift, stemmed from a match in which the Barbarians were not directly involved: Major Stanley's XV against Oxford University played in October 1975. This long-established annual fixture is played as part of Oxford's preparation for the University Match, and usually Stanley's XV comprises top players, who are specially picked to give the undergraduates a thorough examination. Thus the Pontypool Front Row were asked to play at Iffley Road, the invitation being sent directly to Bobby Windsor, from Nigel Starmer-Smith, whom we thought was a member of the match organising committee.

I was a student at that time, but Bobby and Charlie had to take time off from work for the match, played mid-week. It was understood, though, that as with all representative fixtures, we would receive travelling expenses. Players give little thought to the mechanics of the operation. Usually they are asked how much their journey cost and the money is handed over. It is a simple, established procedure.

As we were all travelling from roughly the same area, we

decided to go in one car, which Bobby had borrowed for the day. There is nothing unusual in this. Players who attend squad sessions and representative matches often travel together, if they come from one area or one club, like for instance, the London Welsh players always did when travelling down from London, Pontypool from Gwent or Llanelli from West Wales. It is convenient and sensible. It is also accepted, at every level of the game, that each player claims his own expenses, regardless of the manner of his journey. He claims his mileage and any other costs, such as meals when necessary.

I had no reason to suspect there might be a different attitude on this occasion. Starmer-Smith approached Charlie and me in the changing room after the match to find out our expenses. Naturally we asked the going rate, in other words, the rates the Welsh Rugby Union allowed. Bobby had already received his expenses, but Starmer-Smith declared he would have to get some more cash from the Oxford treasurer to pay mine and Charlie's. It is important to stress that Starmer-Smith did not question the sum we asked. If he objected in any way, or if there was any kind of problem, he certainly did not show it. I'm not sure exactly how much we were paid, but I can say that it was the correct amount for the 100-mile round trip from Pontypool to Oxford. There were no extras, just straight payment for the mileage.

We hadn't a clue that anything was wrong until a month later when Keith Rowlands, chairman of the Welsh selectors, called the three of us to one side after a Welsh squad training session. It seemed there had been a bit of a fuss about our claiming separate expenses for the Stanley's match and that some of the Barbarians committee men were a bit upset about it.

I must say we were shocked by Rowlands' revelation, and we could not understand how or why the Barbarians were involved. Clearly someone at Oxford had complained. Either he was a Barbarian or he considered it necessary to inform the Baa-baas. We never did find out. The situation was, naturally, very embarrassing. We had heard through the grapevine that all three of us had been pencilled in to play for the Baa-baas in the forthcoming match against Australia, and it was also possible that we would be invited to tour with them in Canada at the end of the season. Now it seemed we were taboo. We discussed the situation and inevitably came to the conclusion that from then on we would have nothing more to do with the Barbarians, even though it seemed likely that they felt the same way about us. We were very annoyed about the whole affair, and we made our feelings known.

Bobby Windsor had played for the Barbarians in the last two seasons, while Charlie and I had appeared for them during 1974–75. Suffice to say, there was no call-up for the Australian match or for the Canadian tour. Our Barbarian careers were over, we were sure. Imagine my surprise three years later when contact was re-established a couple of weeks before the Baa-baas were due to play New Zealand in the final match of their 1978 tour. The message came via Ray Prosser, our coach at Pontypool, who had played for the Barbarians in 1958.

'Pricey, the Barbarians committee want you to play against the All Blacks,' Prosser declared, adding that the committee were aware of my feelings towards them. They had asked him to make the initial approach, rather than issuing an invitation direct from the Barbarian secretary, Geoff Windsor-Lewis. I told him that I would not play and so Pross asked me to ring Rhys Williams and talk to him direct. Accordingly I rang Rhys. He said that it had taken a long time to bring me back into favour with the Baa-baas and asked me to reconsider. I told him exactly what I had told Prosser. I had made my decision. There was no way I was going to play for the Barbarians.

A little later, Prosser rang me again. Windsor-Lewis had been in touch with him yet again, asking him to use his influence to persuade me to change my mind. We talked and we talked. I told Pross that I still felt very angry about the expenses business. There was no way anyone was going to cast aspersions on my character over a perfectly legitimate claim. It had become a matter of principle. To turn down the chance of playing against the All Blacks was something not many players will do, but even if the whole of the Barbarian committee,

Herbert Waddell, Windsor-Lewis, the whole gang of them, went down on their knees and apologised, I was determined to stick by my decision. 'Are you going to play?' Pross eventually asked. 'No, definitely not,' I replied. 'Fair enough' said Pross, 'Ta-ta, see you next week'. That was the end of the matter, one of the more disagreeable chapters in my career. It was also the end of the Barbarian connection for Bobby and Charlie. Neither were invited to play again.

This may be the place to recall my first involvement with the Barbarians. The night before they were due to play their first match of the 1975 Easter tour to Wales, against Penarth on Good Friday, I was invited to join the tour party because they had found themselves short of a prop. The go-between was Ray, Prosser. Naturally, I accepted the invitation enthusiastically and duly joined the team at Penarth. I did not play in that match but was told I would be in the team against Cardiff the following day. Charlie Faulkner, an original choice, would also be playing at the Arms Park. It seemed an opportunity not to be missed.

I'm not sure what I was expecting. All I knew, at the time, was that I would be playing for a club with a long tradition and that most players reckoned it an honour to be asked. My introduction was based on pure Barbarianism: a welcome, which at best was patronising, their quaint initiation ceremony and much pontificating about 'the spirit of the game' and their tradition for 'running the ball'. I wish Cardiff had also been inspired with such idealism. I ended the match with studmarks right up my back, the result of a good, old-fashioned raking in a ruck. My back was not the only item shredded. My first Baa-baas jersey was in tatters and I had to change it. Still, it was a Baa-baas jersey and it seemed a worthy item to add to my growing collection of rugby paraphanalia, even though my wife's sewing expertise might be required to restore it to good order. So I asked our worthy Baa-baas committee if I could have the jersey. I might have had a better response if I'd asked for ten West Stand tickets for an England–Wales match. The request was firmly turned down.

In view of all the later fuss with the Barbarians over expenses, it is worth stating that for this, my first involvement with them, I did not demand one penny. It was not possible for me to stay at the team hotel over the weekend so I had to make several trips to and from Cardiff. Perhaps I would have been respected more if I had put in a hefty claim, instead of none at all.

If all the stories concerning expenses were true, I daresay many of Britain's top players would be driving around in Rolls Royces. When I look at my battered 1977 Ford Capri, I reckon I must have missed out somewhere! Five years ago both the Welsh Rugby Union and the RFU clearly began to believe the malicious gossip, and ironically made it much more difficult for players to appear in events such as charity matches. The players, they ordered, must apply to the respective governing bodies for permission to play in any one-off match, regardless of its purpose. On occasions, players were refused permission to play, even in a charity match. This was another example of unwarranted interference with and impingement on the rights of amateur players to play when and where they liked.

The explanation that accompanied the new restrictions was that the authorities were worried that the top players were playing too much. No mention was made of what was clearly their real concern – that players were receiving perks and rewards for matches and endangering their amateur status.

What I will say is that in certain matches, players were treated far better by the organisers than they were by their respective Unions. Not only were there first-class hotels, à la carte meals and a generous travel allowance, but what's more, wives and girl-friends were usually invited and accorded the respect and treatment that would have been a lesson to the authorities. Many players appeared in one-off matches for this reason and this reason alone.

Much depended, of course, on the amount the organisers had at their disposal. But there were many occasions when, because the expenses fund was small, or because the reason for the match was to raise as much as possible for, say, an injured player or his dependants, then expenses to players were kept as low as possible. I have played in several matches where I did not ask for a penny in expenses, notably for the blinded Pontypool policeman, Alan Williams, and the Barrie Lewis Match at Aberavon. At others I asked for a nominal amount only, even though this meant being out of pocket. I want to stress that this was the rule rather than the exception. Rugby players are not money-grabbers, as many people believe. How many know, for instance, that several players who appeared in the Sam Doble Match at Moseley in 1978 received their expenses only to return them to the fund. One of those was J. P. R. Williams, who did not even bother opening the envelope. Bill Beaumont was invited to play in one charity match, but had to withdraw because of injury. So he sent his apologies and included a cheque as a contribution to the day.

Another element of these invitation matches which the authorities overlook is that they are often fun. Players enjoy a break from the rigours of their normal rugby timetable, and if there is a good night out involved, which there usually is, it is an added incentive.

When you see officials, and their wives, enjoying tremendous hospitality on special occasions, and sometimes receiving gifts, you begin to wonder who are the real amateurs in our game. The players are not the only contributors, of course, at one-off matches. Referees often give their services completely free. Some, however, might regret their involvement. I recall one match at Taunton which was refereed by Mike Titcomb, of Bristol. It was a horrible night, rainy and muddy. By the time the match was nearly finished, every player was plastered with mud. Titcomb, dressed all in white, stood out like a beacon, with hardly a spot on him. This proved too much of a temptation for the players. On a given signal, Titcomb was seized and given a mud-bath. By the time he had regained his feet and his composure, the only white visible was the whites of his eyes! Not all the players had joined in. One, Alistair McHarg, decided to use the temporary distraction for his own purposes; he picked up the ball and ran 75 yards for a try. The Scotsman's jubilation, however, was short-lived. Titcomb refused to award the try because, obviously, he was in no position to see it scored.

I don't think McHarg was altogether happy with the explanation!

Talking of charity matches reminds me that the last time the Pontypool Front Row played together was on 28 March 1983. We were picked for the Pontypool President's XV against an Invitation XV in a match at Pontypool Park in aid of the blinded Gwent policeman, Alan Williams. It was supposed to be an entertaining match, with the ball being thrown about as part of the amusement. Only when we were 10–30 down, did we realise that the opposition were taking it rather more seriously. We at once changed our approach, and, by employing 'Pontypool tactics', we won 50–44. What we hadn't been told, was that our opposition, named an Invitation XV, but virtually the Wales B side, were looking for serious match practice and some of them were playing for their places on the forthcoming tour of Spain. I think it was an impertinence to use a charity match in this way.

In the end, the selectors finished up with egg on their face – and serve them right! One of the more interesting aspects of the match was the confrontation between the Pontypool Front Row and theirs which consisted of: Ikey Stephens, of Bridgend, Billy James, of Aberavon, and Rhys Morgan, of Newport. As Ikey and I had been in far more earnest opposition just two days before, when Pontypool played Bridgend in the Welsh Cup semi-final, it was mutually agreed that we would have a comfortable, unpressured match. Bobby, too, had nothing to prove against Billy, even though the Aberavon hooker was Wales's No. 1 (knowing Bobby, though, it might have been tempting to have a go at Billy!). Rhys Morgan, however, must have been in a bit of quandary. It was rumoured that his place for the Spanish trip was on the line. Presumably, he was required to do a good job against Charlie Faulkner, his coach and mentor at Newport. It was like asking me to go on the field against Ray Prosser and give him a good hiding, in a scrummaging sense. The 'non-aggression' pact, however, sensibly extended to Rhys and Charlie, who certainly enjoyed himself. Charlie, in fact, played the whole match, which was not bad for someone of 42 who was supposed to have given up the game.

Memorable Matches

When I played against Llanelli in the quarter-final of the Welsh Cup at Stradey Park on 25 February 1984, it was my 425th appearance for Pontypool, which meant that I had beaten Terry Cobner's record for most appearances for the club. I don't know why but whenever I break some record or other, it always seems to coincide with a day of disappointment. Something always seems to go wrong. It certainly did at Llanelli. Although the result was 15–15, we lost because the Scarlets scored the only try of the match, which meant that the Cup-holders of 1983 were out of the competition.

Looking back over my career, this jinx seems to have struck an inordinate number of times. It would have been easy, of course, to disguise this curious flaw in my record and I could have chosen to describe only those matches in which the side I was playing for won. The defeats could have been conveniently overlooked. However, I have not chosen the following matches for any particular reason other than I hope they provide a representative view of my career with Pontypool, Wales and the British Lions.

My first match for Wales was played in Paris on 18 January 1975. I ran on to Parc des Princes full of excitement and apprehension, thrilled to be winning my first cap but expecting a torrid and dirty match after experiencing the uncompromising French approach during Wales's B international in Toulouse in 1973 (Bobby Windsor still carries the scar from being booted between the eyes when a scrum collapsed in Toulouse). My fear at the way France would play was, however, partly unfounded, if you ignore the fact that Estève peppered Bobby with punches from the second row. Wales, with nine changes and six new caps, won 25–10 which is our biggest-ever Championship score on French soil. We took them to the cleaners in every aspect of the match, and I was particularly pleased with our scrummaging. I was up against Vaquerin the experienced French loose-head, who was a good prop in every sense.

It was also the Pontypool Front Row's first appearance for Wales, for on the other side of Bobby Windsor, Charlie Faulkner was making his début. Azarete, Charlie's opposite number, certainly knew he had been in a game by the end. It was Azarete's twenty-first and last cap, and he was not the only prop seen off by the redoubtable Charlie. The other new boys in the Welsh team were: Steve Fenwick, Ray Gravell, John Bevan and Trevor Evans, and the way they fitted into the scheme of things certainly indicated that Wales had the making of a first-class side. Bevan, who coaches Wales now, was a controversial choice at fly-half, chosen ahead of Phil Bennett. Bevan played well enough to justify his selection and, of course, he benefited from the amount of possession we won and Gareth Edwards' controlled delivery. It is interesting that the side, when originally selected, was given little chance by the critics, who not for the first time had their scepticism thrown back in their faces.

Wales scored five tries and the fact that I got one of them was the icing on the cake for me. Naturally I remember it well, as I don't often get the chance to run 75 yards and score. I also remember vividly that the next Welshman up in support of me was J. J. Williams – who significantly had cut across from the other wing – and, a few yards back, was none other than Charlie. The fact that the try came near the end of the match, when everyone was understandably beginning to flag, speaks volumes for the athleticism of Pontypool Park-trained front-row men! J.J., incidentally, was a vastly underrated player, who rarely received due credit for the many unnoticed contributions he made to a match: he was a relentless chaser of kicks, he ranged across the field, and was quick to cover his opposite wing whenever the opposition were attacking. My try was a case in point – J.J. appeared as if by magic, while Gerald

Davies, on whose side the try was scored, was nowhere in sight.

The Scotland–Wales match at Murrayfield on 1 March 1975 was my first encounter with 'Mighty Mouse'. At the time, Ian McLauchlan was probably at his prime and regarded as the world's best loose-head prop, with a wealth of experience behind him. The challenge of scrummaging against one of the 'greats' in my first international season, was not so much daunting as intriguing. I would find out at first hand what first-class scrummaging was all about and would discover just how I measured up to it. If the situation posed questions, it would certainly provide answers. Some of these I knew already, having watched Mighty Mouse on TV playing for the 1971 Lions in New Zealand, when he had taken over as No. 1 loose-head from Ray McLoughlin after the Irishman had been invalided out of the tour following the Battle of Canterbury. Having taken his chance then, McLauchlan confirmed his ability in South Africa in 1974 when he played his part in destroying the Springboks in the scrum, traditionally their strongest and most formidable part of the game.

A measure of McLauchlan's success against the Springboks was that on one occasion he hoisted Hannes Marais clean out of a scrum – the same Marais who became a living legend in South Africa, such a hero in fact that he was chosen to captain his country. For Marais, then rated the world's No. 1 tight-head, to suffer such an indignity meant but one thing: Ian McLauchlan was a loose-head of exceptional ability. Bobby Windsor, who had played with him in South Africa, confirmed it – and gave me some advice about what techniques the Scot would use. Mighty Mouse, at 5 feet 9 inches was relatively small but he took advantage of his lack of height. He did this by scrummaging lower than his opposite number and by using a dip and lift technique, he would try to unsettle the tight-head and then lift him. There is a limit to how low props can scrummage comfortably, and Mighty Mouse tried to exploit that limit by first going low, then dipping lower again so that the tight-head would be forced to try and ease the pressure. Once that happened, it was much easier for the loose-head to ift and then push the tight-head backwards.

I was determined not to let this happen to me. My countering technique was simple: as I preferred to scrummage low myself, I decided to match him, however low he wanted to go. The result was that he went low, I went low and we both went low together! It proved to be real daisy-cutting, our noses ust off the ground. Not surprisingly, most scrums ended up collapsed. The outcome of our particular match was, I reckon, fairly even (Scotland won 12–10), which gave me a great deal of satisfaction, and pleased Wales too, for in the previous year our forwards had been pushed, wheeled and crabbed at will by the Scots. Mighty Mouse did not give me the same sort of battle in subsequent years, but he certainly ranks among the best scrummagers I have played against and definitely the best loose-head from a technical point of view.

Although the match against Argentina on 16 October 1976 was not a full international and caps were not awarded. Wales played their strongest available side. It was one of the hardest matches I have ever played at the Arms Park, and even though we had some excuse in that the match was rather early in the season and there was a lack of match fitness, we were lucky to win (20–19). Argentina deserved to beat us.

Scotland defeated Wales in 1982 because they scored from our mistakes. But Argentina created their own chances and made the might of Wales look pretty puny. They regularly created overlap situations purely thanks to elementary mistakes in our defence. When playing against so-called emergent countries, you expect to face problems, but more with the opposition's commitment than in the area of skill and ability. We, the experts, should have been teaching them, the beginners, not vice versa, as happened on the day. The match was in injury time, when we saved it . . . or at least Travaglini, their capable centre, did it for us by high-tackling J.P.R. Norman Sanson ordered a penalty but when the Scottish referee's back was turned, Phil Bennett 'stole' five yards to shorten the range. When Benny's kick went over, a great sigh of relief was heard around the ground. No one was more relieved than the Welsh players!

One match infamous in the history of the annual series between England and Wales was the 'Ringer Match', or the 'Battle of Twickenham', played on 16 February 1980. But for me it was, without qualification, the most enjoyable international I have taken part in. A Welshman needs little motivation to play well against England at any time. This time it was special; the atmosphere was electric – it was like playing at the Arms Park – and there was a tremendous feeling of anticipation. I have never experienced anything else like it.

The incidents which led up to Paul Ringer being sent off are well known. There were fast and furious exchanges on both sides in those stormy opening 15 minutes before Ringer was given his marching orders for a late tackle on John Horton, the England fly-half. It was not a particularly dangerous or dirty act; but because it occurred after the Irish referee David Burnett had issued a general warning, Ringer became a victim of circumstance. In another match, in a different atmosphere, the most he might have got was a severe ticking off. Fran Cotton, who was standing near me at the line-out when Ringer launched himself at Horton, was incredulous. 'He must be a head-banger. He can't be right,' he muttered in disbelief. Cotton, like many of us, was amazed that Ringer had even contemplated 'having a go' in such a potentially explosive situation. What I do know was that he was utterly distraught afterwards. It took a long time for the full implication of his act to sink in. It also goes without saying that Wales deserved to win, regardless of what happened. We outplayed England, even with 14 men, and outscored them two tries to nil.

Although I was in the heat of the battle as it were, I cannot honestly say who or what started the chain of events. One newspaper interviewed 29 players – presumably they tactfully did not approach Ringer – and views differed as to the crimes and their perpetrators. Although as I've said, I was looking forward to the match immensely when I went out on to the field, I had no intention of being involved in any unpleasant-

77

ness. At least I didn't go on to the pitch with any purpose other than to play the game of my life. I was booted in the head. But that can happen in any match. Some other players, on both sides, were slightly more aggressive than they would normally be, but it was that kind of match. Certainly when Roger Uttley was kicked in the head on the floor, I believe it was more an accident than a deliberate attempt to injure. Much was made, too, of the 'war' between Terry Holmes and John Scott, club-mates at Cardiff but on the opposite sides this time. I thought it was rather mild stuff, frankly. My only concern was to do my job to the best of my ability, and when Ringer was sent off, I found that was precisely what I had to do. We were down to seven forwards for most of the match, and more than held our own, but this was disappointingly overlooked. Wales lost 8 points to 9.

I am convinced that the press were largely responsible for the build-up of tension before the match. There was talk of dirty play by Wales against France in the previous match, and of how the England front row were going to react if and when I was going to collapse scrums. It went on and on. Personally I could not believe that Fran Cotton & co had anything to do with all this nonsense. If they had anything to sort out, I was sure they would not issue threats via the press, but would sort out their problems on the field. I have since learned that much of the provocation stemmed from Derek Morgan, one of the England selectors. During the week before the match, whenever I spoke to reporters, I genuinely tried to defuse the situation. I felt that all this animosity was not only unfair to the players, but might put undue pressure on the referee. I prayed that the referee would be strong enough not to be influenced by what appeared in the press. However, David Burnett proved a disappointment. He made no attempt to show that he hadn't been influenced by the pre-match build-up. He proved this at the very first scrum when he came around to stand on my side – he should have been watching the put-in on the other side.

Once the dust had settled and both sides got down to the serious business of trying to win the match, it was a marvellous experience. Although it was hard and demanding, everything seemed to happen easily, without effort. I didn't feel exhausted at any stage; the scrummaging was less of a problem than it looked, and the feeling of urgency lasted for the full 80 minutes. It was not until after the game and during the next few days that I realised how much effort had gone into the match and how much physical and nervous energy had been used up. It normally takes me about ten days to fully recover after an international; this time it took far longer, and I believe most of the Welsh team felt the same. It is possible that this was one of the causes of Wales's much poorer performance in the next match, against Scotland, and the following defeat against Ireland.

In retrospect, I think Wales were unfairly singled out as the villains of the piece. Certain members of the Welsh Rugby Union were determined that, as an example, three players should be dropped for the match against Scotland. Fortunately Rod Morgan, the chairman of the selectors, successfully managed to dissuade them, and it would have been a total miscarriage of justice anyway. Rod, however, certainly read the Riot Act at the next team meeting. That 'behaviour' would not be tolerated again. He asked for support and respect from the players because he had put his head on the chopping block by placating the WRU committee. A week before we played Scotland, Jeff Squire, our captain, had a private chat with Rod at his home about the whole episode.

It is interesting to reflect on what happened after the England match, and what preceded the match against France the next year. Before that match, Keith Rowlands, the chairman of the selectors, made it clear that we were not wearing kid gloves. After the match, which was a rough and dirty one, we were told in the changing room that the party-line was to be that it hadn't been a dirty match. A year later, we were again given carte blanche before we went out to play England at Twickenham, this time when Rhys Williams was chairman.

The first Test in the 1980 Lions tour to South Africa was at Newlands, Cape Town on 31 May. It was the old story of the opposition capitalising on mistakes by the British Isles. South Africa scored five tries to one, but even so we were always in the match with a chance of victory. We had the better of the forward exchanges, especially in the loose, and we were far more mobile than their juggernaut pack. Tony Ward, whose 18 points were a record for a Test in South Africa, kept us in the hunt with his kicking, but although we clawed our way back time and again, we let the match slip away 22–26 because we made many silly, elementary mistakes.

A few weeks later in the second Test on 14 June we had the better of the Springboks pack at Blöemfontein, only to give away two tries late in the match. One of the earlier South African tries should not have been allowed. Ray Mordt, tackled by Bruce Hay, passed off the ground, and Willie du Plessis gathered the ball to put in Stofberg.

Then in the third Test at Port Elizabeth on 28 June the Lions gave the Springboks a real pounding in wet, soggy conditions, which should have made us feel at home. We thoroughly deserved to be leading 10–6, only for disaster to overtake us again, this time in the shape of Clive Woodward. The English centre, picked out of position on the wing, could not be held to blame as he didn't have the reactions of a wing. South Africa took a quick throw-in, through Germishuys to Stofberg, and the flanker returned the pass for Germishuys to score a crucial try. If Woodward had reacted like a wing, he would have stood on the five-yard line until the forwards arrived, but instead he ran back to a defensive position, leaving the five-yard line undefended. We lost the match 12–10. On 12 July at Pretoria we finally achieved a result (17–13) which reflected our superiority. It was the first time a Lions side had won a fourth Test in South Africa. The forwards again gave their all; this time we translated it into match-winning points. The real lesson of the Test series, however, was the absence of a true flier in the back row. After losing Stuart Lane only 51 seconds into the first match of the tour, the handicap was obvious in match after match. Colm Tucker strove hard to play that kind of part, but he was not equipped for it. We also made the sort of mistakes that cost us the 1977 series in New Zealand and we were duly punished. The French referees in all four Tests were good, with only the occasional lapse, but the standard of South African refereeing in the other matches was often very poor.

Pontypool versus Australia on 4 November 1981, played at Pontypool Park was, without question, a humiliating defeat; we lost 37–6. Australia played superbly in the back row and at half back, where they continually crossed the advantage line and had Pontypool going backwards for much of the match. Once this was achieved, the Australians had so much speed there was no way we were able to stop them scoring.

Having given the Australians their due, I think it is relevant here to stress the factors which contributed to our defeat. Australia were forewarned by the press that Pontypool would give them their hardest match, outside of the internationals. Our pack, the experts predicted, were going to dominate play. They prepared accordingly, which is to be expected of a touring side. When Wales and the Lions tour, the 'tough' match is always acknowledged, and the touring side raise their game accordingly, as for example: the Taranaki–Lions in 1977, Western Province & Northern Transvaal–Lions 1980. Another factor which helped lead to our downfall was that Australia treated the match as if it were an international, and paid Pontypool the compliment, if that's what it was, of effectively playing their Test side. They even went to the length of seeking the late Carwyn James's advice as to how they could combat our strengths and tactics. As far as my experience of touring was concerned this was unique. We have never sought any local help on any tour (nor indeed expected any). More often than not, we had to stage our training sessions in secrecy to prevent spying, as in South Africa in 1980 when Ian Kirkpatrick, then South Africa's coaching organiser, tried to watch nearly every Lions training session. At one point, you could have been excused for thinking that Kirky was a member of the tour party!

The refereeing was also extremely poor. Roger Quittenton effectively knocked our guts out by awarding a penalty against us for collapsing a scrum early in the match. We had started off strongly and had pushed them off two scrums at which they had the put-in. We were in the process of pushing them a third time when their front row fell backwards over the top of their second row. The scrum collapsed and Pontypool were judged responsible. It was not only a bad decision by Quittenton, but illogical, for having already proved our supremacy in the scrummage, what advantage would we have had in deliberately collapsing the scrum? Rightly or wrongly, you could actually see our boys despair from that moment. We also succumbed to our usual weakness of 'freezing' on the big occasion. Pontypool are such a well prepared side, that this failing is inexplicable and yet it has happened on many occasions. It was probably the biggest contributory factor towards our downfall and the disappointment of it was that we failed to do justice to ourselves or to Ray Prosser.

Scotland had not won at Cardiff for 20 years until 20 March 1982 when they beat us 34–18. I wish they had picked another day to end their dismal run, because it should have been a very special occasion for me. We were sitting in the changing room, moments before kick-off when Gareth Davies, the Wales captain, came up to me and asked if I would be breaking the record that day. I told him that I would, in fact, only be equalling it. I think Gareth was mixing the records up slightly. I had, in fact, passed Denzil Williams's record of 36 caps, which had made him Wales's most-capped prop in the previous match, against England at Twickenham. This time, I would be equalling Mervyn Davies's record of 38 appearances, a record for a forward. Anyway, Gareth was clearly determined that the occasion would be marked. As we entered the tunnel just before running out on to the pitch, he tossed the ball to me. 'Would you like to run out first?' he asked. Talk about passing the buck . . . I led Wales out, all right, to the biggest score ever against Wales on our own soil, our first defeat at Cardiff since 1968, and the end of a run of 29 Championship matches without defeat at home.

The defeat was unbelievable and inexplicable. In fact, in the opening 15 minutes we put Scotland under so much pressure, that I said to myself: 'we're going to give them a real good hiding'. There was a hiding all right. But it was Wales who took it. I can't remember another match in which everything went wrong for one side. It started with a Gareth Davies kick bouncing badly for us and right for Roger Baird . . . it continued with Ray Gravell falling flat on his backside, something he'd never do in another match . . . and it finished with Scotland running in five tries, not one of which they had created for themselves.

The 30th of April 1983 was the greatest day in Pontypool's history . . . we won the Welsh Cup, against Swansea, for the first time, 18–6. The fact that not everyone acclaimed our success did not restrain our celebrations, nor did it diminish in any way the players' tremendous feeling of satisfaction at the success. A great many reports in the press described the match as dull, dreary and boring. We certainly didn't think so! Others declared it a disappointing final. It wasn't disappointing for us, or for our supporters! I can say, without qualification, that we have no apologies for adopting the tactics that won us the match . . . we had not won the Cup before and we were determined to make the most of the opportunity. That we completely out-played Swansea seems to have been lost on the critics.

I really don't know what everyone was expecting. Ian Hall, the Swansea coach, declared before the match that he knew exactly how Pontypool would play. So he couldn't have been disappointed either. Other commentators suggested we should have thrown the ball about and played 'entertaining' rugby. I can suppose only that they wanted us to gift wrap the Cup and give it to Swansea. They played it their way, and lost. The answer as to who was right and who was wrong is contained in the result. We had planned our tactics to beat Swansea and we stuck rigidly to the formula. Having failed to do ourselves justice on the big occasion before, we were determined not to let it happen again, even to the point of being over-cautious.

If our detractors could have seen the look on Ray Prosser's face as we trooped back into the changing room with the Cup, even they may have appreciated what the victory meant to us. After all the trials, tribulations and criticism, and after all his efforts to raise Pontypool's playing standards, this was the most emotional and satisfying moment of his life. To those who failed to applaud or appreciate, all I can say is that we won the Cup as much for Pross as we did for ourselves.

After struggling to find our form in the opening six matches of the 1983 Lions' tour to New Zealand, the first Test was the first occasion that we gave any indication of our capability. We lost 16–12. It was the first time that the Test team had played together, and many aspects of the match showed that we had something to build on. (Compared with the 1977 tour, though, we would still have had three weeks to go before the first Test, and so much more time to arrive at our best team.) Despite the short preparation, we still had the chances to win comfortably, but it was the old story of failing to take them. The loss of Terry Holmes with a knee injury had a devastating effect on the rest of the tour.

In the second Test on 18 June we did extremely well until half-time, only 0–9 down after playing through one of Wellington's famous gales. During the interval, I thought to myself: 'we've really got them now'. The All Blacks, in those first 40 minutes, had shown us precisely what tactics we had to adopt: they belted the ball straight down the middle, even from their own 25, and allowed the wind to do the rest, usually over our deadball line. It not only meant they played much of the first half in our territory, but inevitably we had to drop out the ball back to them. Surely, I thought, we could adopt the same tactics, for the wind was still fierce. Tragically we didn't.

For some reason, we tried subtlety rather than the good old-fashioned big boot, grubbers, kicks into the box, chips through the middle or long punts to the corner. It proved disastrous tactics as the All Blacks dealt with everything with efficiency and confidence. They gave a tremendous, disciplined performance and did not give away one penalty in the whole of the second half. We did not put enough pressure on them. Perhaps we ought to have had a pre-match tactical discussion with their

Wellington experts – Allan Hewson, Stuart Wilson and Bernie Fraser!

Although our defeat in the Third Test, 15–8, on 2 July meant that the Lions had lost the series, it was a very special match for me, because I became the most-capped Welsh Lion. It was my eleventh Test appearance for the Lions, which took me ahead of Gareth Edwards and Rhys Williams. The match was played in appalling conditions, and we were unlucky to have lost, particularly as we scored two tries to one and did well all-round in winning possession. However, in the second-half, we were penned near our own 25 for long periods. We were winning the ball, but we were unable to clear our way into the All Blacks' half.

We were slaughtered in the fourth Test 38–6 on 16 July and what a way to end one's international career! Beaten out of sight by a New Zealand side which took full advantage of the fragile make-up of the 1983 Lions. The only consolation, for me, was that I became the only Welshman to have appeared in all the Test matches on three successive Lions tours and so my career finished after 53 international appearances, a record for a prop forward. However, I would have given half of those caps away to have been on a Lions side which thrashed the All Blacks by a similar margin.

Touring

In comparison to some rugby jet setters who have toured in as many as 20 countries, my touring has been rather mundane, at least in the number of countries I have visited. But I would not have swapped places with anyone, and I count myself lucky to have been a part of tours that have been marvellous and meaningful for their rugby. Apart from an exceptional trip to Germany with Pontypool in 1983, when I made up the party but did not play, all my tours have been inspired by an eagerness to play rugby at the highest level. For me, touring has been a rich and fulfilling experience, and if sometimes the results did not live up to personal expectation, the enjoyment and satisfaction always outweighed the disappointments.

Having played representative rugby in Australia, Fiji, Hong Kong, Japan, New Zealand, South Africa and the USA, I am something of an old hand at the tour game. I'd like to think those tours were part of my education and that I learned something from each one of them. I may not be qualified to write a rugby tour brochure of do's and don'ts, but touring has broadened my view of the world, and taught me to appreciate that sport, and particularly rugby, is a great bridge-builder, forging friendships that hundreds of political summit meetings could never hope to achieve. Let me say at once, I am not a political animal, but as a rugby player I strongly resent the intrusion of politics into my private life and leisure pursuits. You can't pick up a newspaper nowadays, it seems, without some threat, some boycott, some blacklist aimed at rugby players. I play rugby because I enjoy it. I also feel that as a member of a so-called free, democratic society, I have the right to choose where and when I play my game. It has nothing to do with politics. I may hold private views on the apartheid system in South Africa, the Junta in Argentina, repressive regimes in South America and the Soviet Union, but that is my business. It is also my affair, and no one else's, if I choose to play rugby against rugby players from those countries. Let me also stress that if I play against a country whose political system I fundamentally disagree with, it does not mean that I am condoning their Government, or burying my head in the sand or turning my back on human rights.

No rugby player deludes himself that by not playing against these countries he is in any way going to change their political system. That is the greatest misconception of those who would have rugby men jump on to the isolationist bandwagon. It is also about time the rugby authorities realised that the players are heartily fed up with the game being used as a political football; cancelling tours because of outside pressure is an abdication of their responsibility. They should also remember that boycotting rarely works. You have only to look at what happened when the United States and other countries withdrew from the Olympic Games in Moscow because of the Soviet Union's invasion of Afghanistan. The Games still went ahead and the Russians are still in Afghanistan. The American athletes were the losers. It would be precisely the same thing if all sporting links with South Africa were severed – there would be not one iota of political change in the Republic. If the politicians really wanted to influence affairs, they could wield enormous power by imposing economic sanctions.

South Africa is a superb country for the rugby tourist. Certainly it is my favourite port of call as the rugby, hospitality, climate, and the variety of things to see and do, are all excellent. I have visited South Africa four times and each trip was memorable. I serve notice here that, though my international career is over, I am open to any invitation to tour, particularly if it is to the Republic! There have been many noticeable improvements since I first went there, five years ago, but I am not convinced that any of them came about because of South Africa's sporting isolation. While I have great sympathy for the plight of the black South Africans, I cannot see that their lot would be improved by the decision of one sportsman or a group of sportsmen not to go there. It seems totally hypocritical to me that the British Government, for instance, advises our sportsmen to stay away from South Africa, but at the same time they are determined to maintain all other links.

Hypocrisy over South Africa is not confined to the politicians. The President of the Rugby Football Union, J.V. Smith, made a (presumably personal) statement that he did not believe in maintaining contact with South Africa. After attending the series of matches to celebrate the reopening of Ellis Park, Johannesburg in July 1982, President Smith said he went only on the instructions of the committee of the RFU. If he felt so strongly about it, I am sure he could have found some way of avoiding the embarrassment of going. In any case, he went and along with other world rugby leaders, not only accepted South Africa's lavish hospitality, but also generous gifts. The acceptance of such gifts contravened the amateur Laws of the game, and gave England's players food for thought when the RFU appointed Smith to conduct an investigation into alleged boot money payments. I don't know whether any England player accepted money for playing in Adidas kit, but I do know that J.V. Smith accepted a gift, the value of which would have kept a rugby player in boots for quite a few seasons!

My first tour to New Zealand, with the 1977 British Lions, was a hard slog, in the playing sense. I played in 14 matches, including all four Tests. Only Ian McGeechan (15 matches), Willie Duggan (16), Andy Irvine (18), Gareth Evans (17), Doug Morgan (15) and Fran Cotton (16) played in more. I was on the losing side only three times, all against New Zealand, and I still don't know why we didn't win those three as well. The Lions forwards were so much better than the All Blacks and yet we failed to translate our superiority into points. It was galling.

New Zealand is a fascinating country, with a great variety of things to do and places to see. The main trouble on the 1977 tour was the weather. It was wet, windy and cold for most of the time and this understandably got the players down. Even so, I was disappointed with some of the team's attitude. They became homesick and did not hide it. The malaise was not confined to Welshmen, either. They were missing out, of course, because of their surprisingly negative attitude. Having made the sacrifices in fitness and preparation for the tour, they should have made a bigger mental effort to convince themselves they were going to enjoy everything, come what may. Maybe future Lions tours should think about taking a psychologist along with them!

The weather was not the only debilitating factor on that tour. Although overall, it was enjoyable, there were disturbing features in the attitude towards us displayed by the New Zealand public and by the New Zealand Rugby Union. 'Go home Pommie bastards' was a common cry at most grounds, but the hostility did not end there. Beer cans and even oranges were thrown at us, and after our win in the second Test at Christchurch, a couple of our players were assaulted as they left the field. New Zealanders take their rugby rather seriously. So, too, do the NZRFU, who were very miserly when it came to 'perks' and extras for the Lions. The hotels were poor, rarely better than one-star, the food was cheap and often mediocre and the ration of one bottle of wine (New Zealand produce, of course) between four players on match days showed undue concern for our health. If we wanted more wine or different food, the NZRFU policy was: 'Pay for it yourselves'. Considering that the gate receipts from the first four matches had paid the costs of the whole 25-match tour, this tightfistedness was disappointing. The NZRFU's attitude to finance was summed up in the after-match speech at Auckland by Ron Don, the chairman. Don opened his speech, not with some words of comment on the match, but with: 'I expect you'll all be pleased to know that we had an attendance of 58,000 and the gate receipts were . . .'

Happily, much had changed in all respects when the Lions returned to New Zealand in 1983. There seemed to be a positive attempt by the authorities to make our stay more comfortable and to treat us more generously. Not only was the attitude of the spectators much more friendly, but when the Lions sat down to eat, they were given the choice of à la carte instead of the standard steak, fish or chicken which we had been served for three and a half months in 1977. It was clear, though, that little had altered regarding the money-grabbing schemes of the NZRFU. Our match itinerary was planned not in rugby terms, but in such a way as to wring out maximum gate receipts from the tour. Normal Saturday fixtures against Wellington, Auckland and Canterbury for instance, were switched to mid-week on the premise that these fixtures would ensure capacity attendances. Matches in less strong areas were played on a Saturday because this would command bigger gates than if they were played mid-week.

The most important aspect of touring New Zealand, of course, is the standard of play. There is no such thing as a bad or weak side in New Zealand; the overall quality of their rugby is high, their preparation and commitment excellent. Long may it be that New Zealand provides this challenge to British Lions sides. One day, though, we might learn from the mistakes of previous tours, and allow ourselves a better chance of beating them by more preparation.

Although I have reasons for feeling otherwise, I enjoyed touring Australia, too. Though there was hostility off the field – as well as occasionally on it – a rugby tourist cannot help but warm to the frank, openness of the Australians. Wales had problems there in 1978, but the generosity and hospitality we were shown were important counter-balances.

Even if the International Board's recommendation for pocket money for touring teams had kept pace with inflation, players would still have had a problem in eking out their allowances. It is not readily appreciated how difficult money, or rather the lack of it, is for a player on tour. Although most things on a tour are paid for, the player still needs some degree of financial independence; there are few things more restricting or embarrassing than not having enough money in your pockets. You don't go around on tour with begging bowls exactly, but the system seems to require that you become second-class citizens in financial terms. Many players on Lions tours, for instance, would have had a miserable time but for the generosity of their clubs in supplementing their daily allowances. What is also overlooked is the players' concern for the financial arrangements at home. In 1977, for instance, I was a student and my grant did not cover the whole period I was away. This meant that for nearly two months of that tour, there was no money whatsoever going to my wife, Anne, and our daughters, Joanne, two and a half, and Louise, eleven months. Anne described the situation to a local newspaper as 'a bit of a sacrifice'. Just how much of a sacrifice, few realised.

The hospitality given by the various countries, therefore, assumes greater importance for the player than it probably should. South Africa, as I have said, has no equals when it comes to catering for the player. Another is Japan, where hospitality is part of their culture. Japanese rugby is far from wealthy, but their treatment of tourists is a lesson to the more money conscious rugby countries. With hotel meals, for example, the Japanese Rugby Union set a reasonable limit (4500 Yen) to be charged against the room account. The advantage of that system soon became obvious to the players on the Wales tour of 1975, when after being away from the hotel all day, we quite often 'blew the lot' in one gigantic order for the team room. For those who loved Japanese food, it was quite a feast with a mountain of trays piled nearly 7 feet high! We had other habits. When we arrived back at our hotel after a match or a day of sight-seeing, there would be a race to our rooms to try and be first to order room service. This first come, first served policy worked until the latecomers cannily positioned themselves close to the service lift and hijacked whatever had been ordered!

Dropped

When I was selected to play for Wales against England in February 1983, there was considerable press comment that I was thus to earn my thirty-ninth cap and beat Mervyn Davies's record as Wales's most-capped forward. I'm a pretty phlegmatic sort of person, but I must admit that I felt more than a little pride that I had reached that historic landmark. Understandably many people recognised my achievement, including Hermas Evans, the president of the Welsh Rugby Union: '...he [Price] has been most consistent and loyal, a great contributor to Welsh rugby. He is so willing to play at any time and he is regarded with great esteem in all parts of the world.'

Those words, and the sentiment they expressed, sounded rather hollow less than a fortnight later, when to my absolute horror, the Welsh selectors, using the bluntest axe they could find, chopped me from the team to play Scotland. One moment I was the happiest man in Welsh rugby, the next I was in despair – and, not to put too fine a point on it, bloody angry. Despair because I did not think I played that badly against England, certainly not badly enough to be thrown out, and anger because of the callous way in which I learned that my long run as Wales's No. 1 tight-head prop was over. It would be easy now for me to agree with the view that I should have suppressed my emotions and accepted the decision with, if not good grace, at least without comment. Wiser, more calculating men might have done so. I'm afraid I was not, and am still not of that species. While I must stand by my outburst, in which Richard Moriarty took most of the flack, reflection has since convinced me that with a little more thought and diplomacy, qualities which I then accused others of not having, I could have stated my case better.

Dropped

The background to probably the most controversial incident in my whole career is worth looking at. When I ran on to Cardiff Arms Park to break Mervyn Davies's record, my only thought was to produce 80 minutes of committed play against a country the very name of which sends a wave of eager anticipation through every true Welshman. To play well against England is a desire as inherent in Welsh players today as it was when Wales first met them over a hundred years ago. The England players, I have no doubt, were of like mind, although in their case it may have been more extreme since they were attempting to gain the first English victory on Welsh soil since 1963.

History will confirm the final score as 13–13, which if you are superstitious, was doubly unlucky. Neither side came remotely near to achieving their planned targets of possession, of gain, of scores. Although both teams produced moments of quality play, they were a small part only of a curiously uneventful contest, quite out of character for the match and a long way short of the high expectations of each team's supporters. The post-mortems bewailed the apparent lack of urgency and effort; the absence of inspired play was etched black and gloomy in the newspaper headlines.

Few found anything to praise, others poured scorn. Keith Rowlands, former player and selector, produced the most bitter epitaph: 'The replay's on Tuesday, and I'm not coming'. The players do not have the spectators' advantage of being able to make an overall evaluation of a match. Their view is only a small part of the whole. When a match is bad, or at least when onlookers say it is, the players are sometimes surprised, even incredulous. That some of us consider we have played reasonably well scarcely matters when the entire match is castigated.

This was the case on that bleak, grey day in February and I suppose, to be totally honest, few members of the Welsh side, having heard the boos of the disappointed Arms Park crowd, and then read the newspapers, could have felt certain of keeping his place in the team for the next match, against Scotland. Experience led me to believe that changes would be made, but I reassured myself that I would escape the axe simply because I considered I had played reasonably well. At least I had done my job, and surely the selectors, despite their ignorance of the requisite qualities of front-row play, would acknowledge this? How wrong I was. It is not for me to agree with the incredulity expressed by others when the team to play Scotland was announced and I was dropped for the first time in my career. But, rightly or wrongly, I sensed that some observers understood my indignation, that arose not because I was dropped, which could happen to anyone, but because I was given no explanation for it. I will always see it as an indictment of the selectors that not one of them – not even my Pontypool clubmate Terry Cobner – considered a public explanation necessary. Perhaps they were afraid that whatever reasons they could give, would lay them open to criticism which they would be unable to answer. Perhaps they thought I needed a lesson, a bit of a shake-up. If they thought I was over the top, why didn't one of them have the courage to come up and tell me? In the event, hints began to appear in the press during the following week, suggesting that I was not the committed player I once was. Presumably these hints were 'planted' by the selectors to justify their action. This made by blood boil even more, as I can truthfully say that I have never played for Wales without 100 per cent commitment. I would accept criticism of my technique or performance, but never of my attitude or approach.

It is interesting that the first I heard about the selectors' intention to axe me was via Terry Cobner's wife, Brenda. My wife, Anne, and Brenda were chatting on the telephone two days before the squad session at which the team would be announced when: 'Expect the worst', Brenda told my wife. When I came home from work and was told what Brenda had said, I was puzzled to say the least. The day after the England match, Cobner and I had held a sort of post-mortem at a local club social function in Pontypool. He had said that the team would not be picked until after the following Sunday's squad session, when there would be a full scrummaging trial. They would try out, Cobner added, all the permutations possible in order to establish the best scrummaging pack. As this had more or less come from the horse's mouth – Cobner was after all the squad forwards' coach – his wife's 'revelation' two days before the fact-finding squad session was mystifying.

Anne, quite rightly, insisted I should ring Terry and ask what 'the worst' meant. 'You are going to be dropped', he told me, adding that the selectors held the front five responsible for the bad scrummaging against England. Naturally, I asked him, surely I deserved the benefit of the doubt? I also reminded him that I had told him earlier in the season what the reason was for Wales's poor scrummaging. I was blamed personally, he added, for two collapsed scrums – collapses for which England, not Wales were penalised! It is of incidental importance that five minutes before we took the field against England, Terry had come up to me and said: 'Make sure that you get Moriarty to give you the weight'.

So I attended the squad session knowing what was to happen but intrigued as to how the selectors would deal with it. Surely, I thought, one of them would come up to me, take me to one side and with a few well-chosen words of consolation, break the news? That I could have accepted. Indeed, I would have thought Wales's most-capped forward merited such consideration, if not for loyalty and length of service then out of common courtesy. Not a bit of it. Not one selector, not even Clive Rowlands, the chairman, whose job it should have been, said a word.

The team was read out in the usual cold and matter-of-fact manner during the lunch break, with Ian Eidman, of Cardiff, named as my successor. I think even Ian was shocked, not just because he was going to earn his first cap, but because I had been dropped. I made it my business to congratulate Ian. He said 'thank you', but not much else. There was really nothing else to say. A few of the other players came up to me afterwards and mumbled 'hard luck, Graham', but I had the impression that everyone was a little embarrassed by the whole episode.

Even though I knew beforehand what was going to happen, I still felt shattered by the decision and numbed by the humiliating way in which I had been told of it. My anger at the whole business came later; and when asked the inevitable questions by the rugby press as to why I thought I had been dropped, I blamed poor Richard Moriarty. Let me say at once that my reaction was spontaneous and in no way intended to damage Moriarty's reputation. Not knowing officially why I had been dropped, I suggested to the press that the selectors must have thought that there had been something wrong with our scrummaging against England. If that was the reason, I protested bitterly, then they should lay the blame squarely on Moriarty, as it was obvious to everyone that he was no scrummager. I had carried him, I claimed, and had done so ever since he had first played for Wales; he had not done his job in the scrums, I added, as if that were some unforgivable sin. Of course when these caustic remarks came out in the press, it must have seemed as if I was making Moriarty my scapegoat. Sour grapes, people must have thought. The trouble with the truth is that it often hurts. I'm sorry I failed to recognise that at the time. What I should have said was that it was not Moriarty's fault, but the selectors' mistake for picking him for the second row. Moriarty has many qualities, and a few faults, but even he will admit that he is not a lock forward. He knew how I felt about the situation because after Wales's match against the Maoris on 13 November 1982, I told him quite bluntly: 'I need more weight from you – scrummaging is more important than running about the field.' He replied: 'I don't want to play at lock – I want to be at No. 8.'

Of course he should never have been selected for lock, since the chief purpose of a lock is to give his prop maximum shove and support. Moriarty did not, and could not, as he was a backrow forward pushing in the scrum. Eddie Butler, for example, could get away with the switch from No. 8 to lock, which he did several times for Pontypool, because graft and commitment are part of Eddie's game. When he switched to lock he played like one, totally accepting the requirements of the job. Moriarty was different. He would not really accept them. It must be remembered that I had plenty of opportunity to assess Moriarty's abilities as a scrummager. I had played with him eight times: a Welsh trial, against Australia, four Championship matches in 1982, against the Maoris, and a trial before the fateful 1983 match against England. In the Australia match, Moriarty had made something of an impression, largely because he scored a try and he had tackled a centre with no back-row player in sight. The point is that he had been in a position on the field where no lock forward should have been. He was playing as a No. 8, not a lock. His selection was, after all, a compromise, for at the time Wales were struggling for locks and Moriarty himself played in that position for Swansea only because they were short of locks as well and had too many back-row players. After the Australia match, Moriarty tended to play more and more like a back-row man, when he should have been concentrating on the scrum, maul and ruck. I state frankly that this was a handicap not only for the pack but for the whole side during the time Moriarty played for Wales.

The 1983 England match was not the only one, incidentally, when the selectors chose to criticise our scrummaging. Against Ireland in 1981, we were 'walked' by the Irish pack. The selectors quite overlooked the reason why we went backwards, was because our back row had disengaged. No front five can hold an eight-man shove, and to apportion blame in this instance was absurd.

In the final analysis, Moriarty was one of the many victims of the bad selection which has undermined Wales's attempts to build a good side in recent seasons. If Moriarty was to play for Wales at all, it would have had to be at No. 8. But I could hardly be expected to say so at the time, with my Pontypool captain, Eddie Butler, the man in possession, and Jeff Squire, another Pontypool player, clearly the outstanding candidate to take Butler's place if the need arose.

It is important to remember that I was not the only player dropped after the England match. What about Wales's loose-head, Clive Williams, of Swansea, another player slightingly treated by the selectors? Clive, a late replacement in the squad for the match, fully merited his inclusion, for he was still one of the best technicians in his position in Britain. Not only was he dropped for the Scotland match, but he was booted out of the squad entirely, without a word of explanation or regret, or any acknowledgment of his past performances for Wales. The first Clive learned of it, incidentally, was from his wife, who had heard the announcement on the radio. Players deserve more than that. But perhaps it is not for us to question why selectors behave with such discourtesy.

The ultimate irony of the most extraordinary episode of my rugby life, was the consequence of the reshuffling of the Welsh side. For the match against Scotland, in came my Pontypool clubmates, John Perkins and Staff Jones, for their first caps. Had we done well against England, and the selectors kept their faith in the side, perhaps Perky and Staff would still be waiting for recognition, though I don't think for a moment either of them will thank me by buying my beer every season from now on!

New Zealand 1983

When you fly to New Zealand, the pilot has to be careful or otherwise you're on your way back before you've arrived. If you listen to some people, that's what the 1983 British Isles tourists must have wished had happened to their Air New Zealand Flight No. TE 006 as it made its final approach to Auckland Airport on 7 May; instead throttling up to full power and flying the 12,000 miles home. Had that happenend, then the whole, sad, sorry tour would never have taken place.

The tour, of course, did take place but when we returned we found many who believed that it had been, for some of us, just one ghastly nightmare in which hulking great All Black forwards, mouths afroth, had charged at us brandishing shovel-like fists and stomping all over our poor, frail bodies with size 15 bovver boots.

Rumours were rife, too, of underlying discontent in the ranks, of disillusion with manager, coach and captain, and that the Lions were prevented from speaking their minds. Much of this was exaggerated and far from the truth. I am not for one moment suggesting the 1983 Lions tour was without its problems and disappointments. Nor that some of us did not have regrets.

Overall, my chief memory of the tour is a happy one. Certainly I know of no player who has declared his reservations on this score or who has wished he had not been on the tour. I am not deluding myself about the facts of the tour: we were beaten and beaten out of sight. For some of us, it was a humbling, even humiliating experience. But not because we were defeated by a better side, which we were, but because we all knew, every one of us, we could and should have done better.

What I find most infuriating – as do many of the other players – is that because the team failed in the Tests, a scapegoat had to be found; someone had to take the blame. I realise I am laying myself open to a charge of misguided loyalty, but as far as I am concerned, not one member of the 1983 tour party let any of the others down, or was individually responsible for our failure. Many things contributed towards the failure of the tour.

There is no doubt that the seeds of our destruction were sown long before the tour took place, in the planning of the fixtures, in the failure of British rugby to recognise what is required of a touring party to win a series in New Zealand and what are the ultimate components of the team. It would be naïve of me not to agree that there were players who should have been selected and were not; that the choice of Ciaran Fitzgerald as captain was not unanimously accepted; and that question-marks existed about the temperament and ability of Jim Telfer as coach.

But those matters are entirely the province of the men who organised the tour, selected the management and chose the players. If blame is to be laid, it should be laid there. It seems ludicrous to me to condemn the whole cast, without linking faults in the performance to the author, the stage manager and the producer.

As one of the players in the drama, or rather tragedy, of the 1983 tour of New Zealand, I can speak only as one of those chosen. Like the other members of the party, management included, we were just the choice of others. . . we had no say in the matter. All that was required of us was to accept the invitation and try our best to achieve a result. This we all did, players, captain, manager and coach. Someone has to lose and in this case it was the British Isles.

Let us consider the case of Ciaran Fitzgerald, the man appointed captain. In my view he should not have gone on the tour. I do not mean to be disrespectful to Fitzgerald, as his record as captain and hooker for Ireland in the previous two seasons proved he was good in both respects. Nor have I come to this conclusion with hindsight – I firmly believed before the tour took place that Peter Wheeler should have been the automatic choice for hooker and the position of No. 2 should have been offered among Alan Phillips, Billy James and Colin Deans. The selectors, in my opinion, took a risk in appointing a captain who had had no previous experience of touring as a Lion, which is a totally different proposition to touring with a national side. In the first place, a Lions side is made up of players from four countries, which not only means there are differences on the playing side, but there are bound to be problems off the field because in many cases the players are complete strangers to one another. Only someone who has toured with a Lions team would realise how important this is. The two essential qualifications, in fact, for a Lions captain are that he has already toured at least once, and that there would be no doubts as to his suitability for the Test berth. Fitzgerald did not qualify in either respect.

So, who should have captained the side? There was strong feeling, before the tour, that it should have been Wheeler. He would not have been a bad choice, but the best one in my view, would have been Jeff Squire. However, Jeff had originally stated he would not be available. But once he was persuaded to go, I was not alone in believing that the 'carrot' was the captaincy. He had all the necessary qualifications for the job: he had experience of leading at international level, he had been a Lion previously and there would have been no reservations about his Test place. Squire was one of the few world-class players in Britain, which would not only have made him accepted but also respected by the rest of the tour party. Wheeler, in contrast seems to have missed out because of the English selectors' whim not to appoint him Bill Beaumont's successor as captain. Peter also expressed some pretty forth-right views which probably didn't help his cause either. Speaking one's mind does tend to upset some people in rugby!

As it turned out, the choice of Fitzgerald was generally applauded by the critics – and it was those same critics who crucified him in New Zealand. Still, I was amazed that Wheeler was not even considered second best by the selectors. There can be little substance in the argument that by taking Wheeler, it would have put pressure on Fitzgerald for the Test place. Impressive displays by Deans in New Zealand must have been an embarrassment if that was the original reasoning for leaving Wheeler behind. Those who eventually called for Fitzgerald's head, blaming him for the poor throwing-in to the line-outs, for his lack of inspiring leadership, for his failure to respond to the suggestion that he step down for the last two Tests, overlooked one important thing: I don't believe the players thought it would have been good for morale if he had stepped down. Certainly I didn't.

The qualities which Fitzgerald did reveal on the tour are also ignored by those looking for a scapegoat. His 100 per cent commitment, his bravery and determination far outweighed his weaker points and, speaking as a prop of a hooker, there were only a few occasions when Ciaran did not do his job properly or efficiently. I would be happy to have Fitzgerald in my side any time. He may not be the best hooker I have played with or the best captain I have served under, but he was my captain and hooker in New Zealand, and nothing happened there to change my loyalty or regard for him. He revealed outstanding patience and tolerance in face of all the criticism, an eloquent testimony to his character.

My one reservation concerning Fitzgerald was that he never gave the impression of being very sure of himself or even in control of the players. This could have been because of inexperience. But my overriding impression was that his hands were tied, that he was just an expression on the field of the power and wishes of Jim Telfer. It was a sort of captaincy by proxy – in my view the captaincy was off the field rather than on it, where it should have been. Everything was prearranged, or so it seemed. I'm not saying it was the same plan for every match, but had I been in his position I would have said what I thought if our plan, our approach was wrong.

A captain must always be allowed to call the shots on the field, to make the decisions, in other words to stamp his personality on the play. Fitzgerald, in this respect, was inhibited, his ideas and individuality constrained by his superiors. A good captain must be able to maintain the urgency and momentum when things are going well, and be allowed sufficient flexibility to change patterns of play and strategy when things are going wrong. These are on-field decisions. I have a feeling that Fitzgerald's decisions were cut and dried for him off the field, with the result that in certain matches we were committed to a style of playing which, when it was not working to the Telfer blueprint, required the captain to make an on-the-spot decision to change tactics. Fitzgerald did not. It was as if he was looking over his shoulder, into the stands, where the Lions' policy-maker was sitting, and saying: 'Look, I'm doing what you've told me.' The frustration of such a situation is obvious. Fitzgerald, who had been chosen in the first place largely because of his influential captaincy of Ireland in the previous two seasons, seemed to me a captain without conviction in New Zealand. It might never have become apparent if we were a winning side: because we were not, the disadvantage was exposed.

Most of the criticism of Fitzgerald focused on his indifferent throwing-in at the line-outs. Some of the critics said this aspect of his play was appalling. This was an exaggeration. I admit he wasn't as accurate as he should have been, but it couldn't have been very bad because we won a fair amount of line-out ball in all four Tests. Ciaran's worst performance, in this respect, was during the third Test at Dunedin. He just couldn't get it right. Even so, we still won a fair amount of line-out possession. I don't think many people realise that the referee in this third Test, Dick Byers, warned him for not throwing straight and then penalised him for it. Even after that, Ciaran's accuracy didn't improve, and I suppose a case could have been made to send him off for persistent infringement. What I do believe is that too much was made of Fitzgerald's throwing-in. The whole thing was exaggerated; the reporters got their teeth into it and wouldn't let go.

Ciaran has played for Ireland since 1979 and he seems to have done a good job for them. It seems odd that his ability was never questioned then. In New Zealand, our line-out jumpers moaned a bit about his throwing-in, but they do that anyway, whether they are playing for their club or their country. What they were complaining about, of course, is that when the throwing-in is not spot on, they cannot perform to their full potential. I know there was much talk about finding someone else to throw-in. But that would have been absurd. Who was going to do it? Me? The wing? A back row forward? A completely new strategy would have had to have been worked out, simply to accommodate one small change in the general scheme of things. It would have been totally impractical.

I have been asked many times, since coming back from New Zealand, what I thought of Fitzgerald's ability. Each time I have replied that it was not my concern whether or not he was the best hooker in Britain. He was picked as captain and he was picked to do a job, which means that if he was good enough to be on the tour he was good enough to play. All the talk about him being dropped – or dropping himself – for the last two Tests did not take account of the consequences. It could have been disastrous for team morale had the captain dropped out. Anyway, I don't believe it was ever seriously considered that Ciaran should not play. Take away his poor line-out throwing, and what do you have? Ciaran never really played a bad game, he was committed and courageous and he always put everything he had into the game. The players respected him for that. He won a lot of friends in the Manawatu game, in which he took a bit of stamping. Many players would not have come back after that, but he did, and was still in the thick of things. He had guts and commitment and on tour those qualities should never be overlooked.

None of this alters the fact that Fitzgerald's selection was wrong in the first place. The blame should be levelled at those who selected him, not the player himself. As a player, I was surprised at some of the choices which were made, because it seemed there were better qualified players left behind. What I am certain of is that John Perkins, my team-mate at Pontypool, should have toured. Although he is not a giant lock forward, his commitment, his two-handed jumping and his scrummaging would have been extremely useful. We needed that kind of hard, grafting, fearless player in New Zealand – and Perky would have been a great asset off the field with his singing, good humour and high spirits.

One of the interesting features of touring New Zealand is the contrast in style and attitude of the respective press battalions. If there is ever a situation when it's 'ours' and 'theirs' it is certainly emphasised there. New Zealand's press coverage understandably favours their players: if one of their players makes a mistake, say, misses a tackle or throws a bad pass, the New Zealand press don't slate him for it. The British press are completely different. They give our players hell, and I can tell you there is nothing more depressing for a player on tour than to read how atrociously he has played. It's bad enough having selectors who are convinced of their divine knowledge: having the press as judge and jury has had more than one player doubting a reporter's legitimacy.

I have been reasonably fortunate in the press I have received. But some of the players can't take it, and get very upset which must be a bad thing, for morale if nothing else. You read patronising articles in the British press about loyalty – yet when do they show it? They pretend to be on your side, but all the time they are sharpening their knives and preparing to stab you in the back. The British press seem to want it both ways – they claim their right to be an integral part of the tour, as long as they can maintain their independence and so-called objectivity when it comes to criticism. No one was more aware of this than Willie John McBride and part of the reason why he was so harshly criticised was that he saw it as part of his job to protect the players from the press. This is an essential part of the manager's job on tour, and has been on every tour I have been on. But when Willie John did it in New Zealand, up went the cry that the players were being gagged. They weren't being allowed to speak their minds, and so on. This was pure fiction, a fabrication by certain members of the press to justify, presumably, to their editors their failure to nail a particular story or inability to find any player to agree with their view. One thing I am certain of: Willie John, as manager, had his priorities right. Everything he did was aimed at taking the pressure off the players and looking after them – he was the sort of middleman between the players and the press.

The policy I suppose did not suit certain reporters. Willie John made it clear from the beginning that if a reporter wanted to interview a particular player, he first had to approach the manager. Willie John, thus commissioned, would then approach the player and ask him if he was willing to talk to the press. If the player declined to be interviewed, his decision was communicated to the reporter. It was as simple and reasonable as that. Yet Willie John was accused of preventing players from talking to the press. Freedom of speech was outlawed, they declared indignantly. I even heard that one writer, someone I regard highly in fact, had described Willie John as a 'total disaster' in his handling of the press and other administrative responsibilities. That was not only insulting and malicious, but also untrue. Possibly there was a lack of communication, or even diplomacy, in some cases, although many of the players felt that the press deliberately did not understand what Willie John was trying to do. Most players on a tour are not worried about talking to the press – some of them enjoy having the rapport – but there are some who positively hate giving an interview. Mistrust plays an important part in this, for all players know that caution must be the byword with certain rugby reporters. They simply do not trust them.

There were plenty of examples of this. One reporter filed a story which suggested that not only were the players not getting on with each other, but on one occasion the animosity between them flared up into a punch-up on the team bus. It was an outright lie. I don't suppose we would have known anything about it, had not Dusty Hare rung home and been told (I think by his father) what had been written. To say the Lions were angry was an understatement, and the reporter who wrote it soon got the message. In any event, he was soon conspicuous by his absence. I believe he even changed his travel plans so that he did not have to face us on an aeroplane or on a bus. I think he knew he'd get a pretty rough reception – it was the same reporter who'd been sent to Coventry by the players during the 1977 tour of New Zealand. It makes you wonder why his editors keep sending him on tours. It certainly can't be for the quality or accuracy of his reporting.

Rugby players are no different from others who perform in public: they appreciate reading that they have done well, but are understandably disappointed when the criticism is less favourable. It is a matter of acceptance, I suppose, and the longer you have been involved in the game the more you realise that there is very little you can do about it. You cannot answer back. The real problem, however, is not the occasional bad review, but not being able to correct an inaccurate statement. If there is one thing which infuriates all players, it is a report based on inaccuracies – and knowing that the person who has written it not only knows very little about the game, but has no affection for it. I'm surprised by the number of reporters covering rugby who belong to this category. Looking back over my rugby career, I can thank my lucky stars, I suppose, that I have had a fairly good press. I can't think of an occasion when my hackles have risen at what I have read about myself. Perhaps I have been fortunate. More likely, though, is that I have 'escaped' because, unlike a threequarter or a back-row player, my contribution is largely unseen. Being an anonymous labourer does have its compensations. It also has its drawbacks in so far because a lot of our work is unseen, it is difficult to disprove criticism.

If I have any complaints in this department it is finding myself quoted when I have never even spoken to the journalist who has written the story. One writer, particularly, has a habit of quoting players without speaking to them, which he might find difficult to verify as he is notorious for leaving matches some ten minutes before the final whistle. And his reason is not to get to the bar before anyone else either!

Not all the reporters are like that. I suppose each player has his number one enemy as well as writers they respect and like.

At home, I get on well with Robin Davey of the *South Wales Argus*. On tour, Brian Madley and John Kennedy took the trouble to come up and inquire about the details of a match. Terry O'Connor was another who was well-respected. You didn't always agree with his viewpoint, but he never failed to come and chat to the players. I'm not sure how players regarded writers like Clem Thomas and John Reason, for instance. You never saw either of them, except on match days, and Reason is notorious for talking to players and always forming his own opinion, regardless of the facts. I have no doubt Clem is very knowledgeable about certain aspects of the game – but I can tell you this, he knows very little about scrummaging.

After the second Test, for example, he came up to me and declared that our scrum had disintegrated. I think he said it was the worst Lions' performance he had ever seen for this. Well, with all due respect to someone who had captained Wales and was regarded as one of the top players of his generation, he didn't know what he was talking about. The incident he was referring to was when the All Blacks wheeled a scrum and we failed to clear the ball. If Clem understood anything about scrummaging, he would realise there is very little that can be done to prevent a wheel against you, apart from being clair-voyant, since the wheel happens so suddenly that the damage is generally done before the players have a chance to react. We certainly didn't disintegrate. To me that means going back-wards which we didn't do once during any match in New Zealand. No side was capable of doing that to us. The only way the All Blacks could put pressure on us in the scrum was to employ the wheel. Their front five forwards were not terribly good at scrummaging, a fact they realised themselves and so worked out an alternative. If we'd listened to some people, the All Blacks' forwards were world-beaters. They were far from that. I was up against John Ashworth and without wishing to be disrespectful, he could never even start to give me trouble, because he simply wasn't good enough as a scrummager. Our problems started in the back row. The All Blacks quickly found out that we had difficulty in getting the ball away, and this was the weakness on which they concentrated their efforts. Disintegrated? Rubbish. If anyone gave way in the scrums, it was New Zealand. We trundled them backwards on quite a few occasions, perhaps not as spectacularly or as consistently as we did in 1977, but back they went, though they still managed to clear the ball. All this is forgotten, of course. What is remembered is that whereas we did not use our possession, the All Blacks did.

I'm not really criticising the press in this respect. The majority of them do their job to the best of their ability. The point is that very few of them have any idea what is happening in a scrum, or what the front five forwards are achieving. This is hardly their fault. Some of the writers I know have never even played the game, a few have played at a low level and those who played internationally were usually backs. I can't think of anyone writing regularly on the game who was, for instance, a front-row forward. With the best will in the world, how can the players be expected to respect someone who doesn't know anything about one of the most important aspects of the game? There are some writers, of course, who played at a high level say 20 years ago. The game today is vastly different, and judgements based on play of their day are totally irrelevant.

There were times when I thought – as one of the senior players – that I ought to attempt to reassure Fitzgerald about the bad press he was getting. I did talk to him, but he was under so much pressure already that eventually I thought it best for him to work it out himself. He appeared to be bearing up quite well in the circumstances. After all, he was an international player and must have learned, by then, how to shrug such things off. If you don't you can easily become paranoid about it.

If you believe everything you read in the rugby press, the 1983 tour was full of bad feeling. All I can say is that we had a very good tour party, and even though a number of the players were disheartened, they made a marvellous job of hiding it. I've been on three Lions tours and considering our poor results I think it was fantastic the way the players kept their spirits up. Whatever else we were, the 1983 Lions were a happy outfit. I would even go so far as to say they were the happiest touring party I have been with.

I'm sure the Four Home Unions have already held an inquest on the tour. I hope that the length of the tour was high on the agenda – because, beyond a shadow of a doubt, this tour proved one thing: ten weeks is far too short a time for a team to build up a chance of winning a four-Test series in New Zealand. At least, the Tests could be reduced to three in order to allow more time before the first Test. A British Isles team is at a disadvantage right from the 'off'. We are a collection of individuals, often poles apart in playing experience and attitude, let alone as products of widely differing coaching methods. To weld us into a side with a definite style of play, with a common policy and attitude, takes time – and time is not what we were given. We had hardly got to know each other, let alone recognise skill or ability, before we were thrown straight into the first Test, just three weeks after arriving.

It was a case of making the best of a disastrous fixture arrangement, one which ideally suited New Zealand, but took no account of our requirements. Those early fixtures were against some of the strongest provincial sides in New Zealand, which meant we had to play demanding matches when we should have been playing sides against whom we could build up our confidence and improve our teamwork. Players had little time to adapt their play to the different requirements of playing against New Zealand teams, with the result that by the first Test our team and our pattern of play was little more than a compromise. That a makeshift XV very nearly won that first Test – and indeed created enough chances to have done so – was a miracle.

There were some misconceptions, particularly back in Britain, about our level of fitness. We knew when Telfer was appointed that he was likely to work us very hard in training in order to attain a high standard of fitness. I thought that this would be a good thing, because of the advantage it would give us over New Zealand. On all my tours, we have started training hard and gradually wound down. This time it did not happen.

Although we attained a high level of fitness, it did not come out in the matches themselves simply because the adrenalin factor was not as high as it should have been. The players were stale because of too much training.

One Scottish threequarter had declined to tour because he knew what we were in for – he didn't want to train every day. He was wrong, as it turned out. We had four days off (out of 70) and one of those contained eight hours of travelling! One of those rest days was granted (albeit grudgingly) after some of the senior players had complained of feeling jaded. Anyway, after this concession our coach started the next team talk (before the Canterbury match) with: 'Right, you've had a day off training. Is anyone stale now?' As if one day off from training would suddenly revive us and start the adrenalin flowing. Telfer had completely missed the point.

During the 1977 and 1980 tours we had developed training routines and patterns which helped to maintain our enthusiasm for the matches. This was evident in that some of our better performances came late on both tours. In 1977, for instance, John Dawes read the situation perfectly. He allowed those players who did not want to train, to lie in if they chose. He reasoned that players were not going to get any fitter and the teamwork was not going to get better. On both tours, we never trained on Sundays. In South Africa, we also did not travel on a Sunday, unless it was the week of a Test match. Those tours usually comprised training in the morning, travelling in the afternoon, with team meetings usually before training unless something special needed to be discussed. In that case, they were always over before dinner. This schedule allowed time for everything: time to train, travel, relax and rest. By the end of the 1983 tour, the players had had enough of Telfer's disciplinariasm.

Compare the last Tests of all three tours: in 1977 we got the adrenalin going to come within a point of beating the All Blacks and in 1980 we made a tremendous effort to beat South Africa. In 1983 we had nothing to give. We felt completely drained. On the field we had no urgency and our reactions were slow. The

All Blacks, faster in thought and action, gave one of the finest displays I have witnessed, and even though their opposition were not up to much, I don't wish to detract from their performance that day.

Old hands like myself saw the warning signs long before the Christchurch Test. I had my doubts after the first week of the tour, particularly about the preparation for the matches. I believe a coach at international level should be more of a co-ordinator than a coach of technique. He should be flexible enough to adopt an approach based on the strengths and weaknesses of the players available, and the one which the majority of players preferred. Telfer was far too rigid. He wanted everything his way. Take, for example, his decision to play our centres inside and outside (similar to New Zealand's 2nd five-eighth and centre) rather than the left and right system they were used to (and preferred). At the line-out, too, Telfer went against the grain by using the prop to 'sweep up' instead of what we had all been used to, that is, using the hooker. When his method had been proved not to work, he allowed us to revert, but then as a variation only.

The biggest failing, though, was that we had had no opportunity to even establish a Test side. The prospective Test side should have played together regularly, and the only way that could have been done successfully was for the touring party to be split into Saturday and mid-week sides right from the beginning. This way, the Test team would have developed teamwork and rapport, not only because they were used to playing together but also because they would have been training together as a unit. Regardless of the varying skills of the players, teamwork would have improved, and that would have been a major factor when confronting the better-prepared All Blacks.

Every touring team has to face up to the problem of injuries. They are bound to occur, and usually with a small reshuffle they do not affect the overall team. However, this time the injury list was disastrous. The loss of players of the stature and class of Holmes, Squire, Stephens and Norster considerably weakened

ABOVE Perhaps not in the Gareth Edwards mould but a pass is a pass for all that. Wales had a narrow shave in this match, against Argentina, at Cardiff Arms Park on 16 October 1976, winning 20–19 thanks to a Phil Bennett penalty goal in injury time. *Colorsport*

ABOVE Bill Beaumont grabs Geoff Wheel as Allan Martin and Phil Blakeway (*right*) intervene, one of several contentious incidents in the 1980 England-Wales match. *Mike Brett*

ABOVE Lending some assistance to Richard Moriarty at a line-out during the Wales-France match at Cardiff Arms Park in 1982. *Colorsport*

ABOVE A moment to reflect during the England-Wales match at Twickenham on 6 March 1982 when the Welsh failure to dominate the scrummaging was a factor in our defeat by 17–7. *Sport and General*

ABOVE Staff Jones and I get a good grip on 1983 Tour captain, Ciaran Fitzgerald, at a scrum in the Second Test between New Zealand and the British Lions on 18 June 1983. *Colorsport*

ABOVE Getting some much-needed protection from my British Lions' team-mates, (*left to right*): Iain Paxton, Jeff Squire, Robert Norster and Maurice Colclough during the First Test at Christchurch on 4 June 1983. *Bob Thomas*

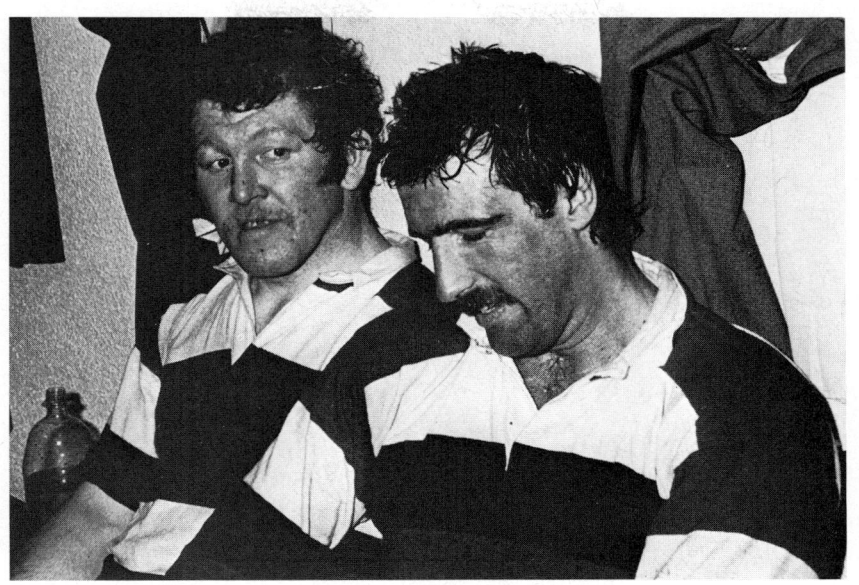

ABOVE The sweet taste of success. With Jeff Squire after Pontypool had won the Welsh Cup at Cardiff Arms Park on 30 April 1983.

LEFT That's torn it! Terry Cobner, now a Welsh selector, changing his shorts during the Sam Doble memorial match in 1977. *Colorsport*

ABOVE LEFT John Perkins, the Pontypool and Wales lock-forward. Perky compensates for his lack of height and brawn with a commitment and two-handed line-out technique few other British locks can match. *Colorsport.* ABOVE RIGHT David Bishop, who staged a remarkable come-back after breaking his neck, to become Pontypool's scrum-half. *Mike Brett*

ABOVE John Dawes, captain of the British Lions in New Zealand in 1971, coach there in 1977 and now National Coaching Organiser of the Welsh Rugby Union.

ABOVE Eddie Butler, one of the most underrated back-row forwards in Welsh rugby. *Mike Brett*

RIGHT Staff Jones, my front-row colleague at Pontypool, who won a place on the British Lions' tour of New Zealand in 1983 after being selected by Wales earlier in the year. *Mike Brett*

ABOVE John Bevan, Wales' National Coach. *Colorsport*

the team. How good would the All Blacks have been if, for instance, they had lost Loveridge, Mexted, Knight and Haden?

I cannot stress strongly enough the enormous pressure there was on the players the whole time we were in New Zealand. Rugby was rammed down our throats from the moment we arrived until we packed our bags after the numbing 6–38 defeat in the fourth Test at Auckland. We were punch-drunk with it, and to be honest, the biggest failure of the tour was that Willie John and Telfer did not recognise the problem. Willie John did try to take some of the pressure off the players by cancelling invitations to functions and the like, only for Telfer to reintroduce the pressure by using the time for team meetings and video sessions. I don't care what attitude players have, how keen they are on playing, but there is no way they can live and breathe the game as if nothing else exists. It was easily the worst tour I have experienced in this respect, our leisure time and 'get away from it all' pursuits seeming just after-thoughts. Part of the fun of touring is seeing the country in which one is playing, meeting the people and having some fun. Such things sharpen one's appetite for playing, because the worst enemies for a tourist are boredom and staleness.

A typical day in New Zealand 1983 was to travel in the morning, have lunch, train in mid-afternoon, sometimes for up to two and a half hours, have dinner and then attend a team meeting to watch video recordings of the Tests and other tour matches. We simply were not allowed to escape from this routine which was not only monotonous, but totally ill-conceived. All travelling, training and TV made the 1983 Lions very dull boys indeed. A typical example of this was our preparation for the second Test. On the Wednesday before the match we travelled from Masterton to Wellington in the morning, and after lunch trained until dark. After training, Telfer said he wanted a meeting that night with the Test team to discuss our preparations apart from training. He suggested that we watch the video of the first Test – to watch and then discuss the first half after dinner on Thursday and the second half after dinner on Friday. I spoke out against the plan, suggesting we leave both evenings free. The video sessions, I thought, should be held in the mornings before we left our hotel for training. In this way we could discuss the match and then put what was needed into practice immediately afterwards. My idea was to shorten the day, instead of dragging the process out for so long. Telfer, somewhat reluctantly, agreed. I thought he had got the message and that for the remainder of the tour, our days of preparation would be more considerate to the players, and the video sessions would be held in the mornings only. However, the following week in Whangarei, after travelling in the morning and training in the afternoon, Telfer said he wanted a video session of the second Test after dinner that evening. Clearly, he had not got the message after all. Fortunately, the facilities for a video were not available and the session was cancelled.

Allowing that there must occasionally be exceptions, it's my view that loyalty to one's fellow tourists must always predominate, and that whatever one may personally think of the lack of ability, say, of any particular player, that opinion should remain unexpressed, a private matter for discussion between the individuals concerned. There were players, who in my view should not have been on the tour, and there were others whose commitment and attitude were questionable. As far as I am concerned, they will remain anonymous. I have no such reservations, however, about the non-playing members of a touring party – management, the coach and the press. I have already commented on two of these elements and I have left the coach to last because in the final analysis it is his philosophy and approach against which the tour has to be measured and judged. Jim Telfer, I believe, was a failure, though not an entirely harmful one for I am convinced that his mistakes will lead to a thorough re-examination of what is required for future Lions tours.

A great many coaches, good and bad, seem unable to distinguish fact from fiction which is not such a bad thing really because a lot of fun can be had from working with such a person. It's only when monomania begins to take over that the problems start. To say that Telfer was obsessed with rugby is an understatement. He seemed to me to be living it every moment of the day – and it wouldn't surprise me if he dreamed about it as well. I'm not criticising his dedication, but I think he lost sight of what the game is all about – it's a game for the players and in all matters the players must come first. By the end he had become known as the Video King. What I didn't like was the manner he adopted – we were like a bunch of schoolkids and he was the schoolmaster, pointing to the video and chiding us for our mistakes. It's not at all surprising that the players felt constrained. They became terrified of making mistakes and some of them went on to the field determined not to put themselves in a position where they might make a slip. It was absurd, and it was a major factor in our failure to produce top-quality performances.

The total disregard for the opinion of the players, especially the senior ones, was another of Telfer's faults. A good coach is one who is prepared to listen to players and, if not totally accept their views, at least show a willingness to incorporate them or try them out. After all, it is the players who have to use the methods. Telfer listened all right. But then he went ahead with his own ideas. This had not happened on previous Lions' tours. Each successive Lions tour has always been a sort of extension of the previous tour, with the older hands like me, better able to understand what was needed because of our previous experience. We knew what should and shouldn't be done. Telfer took no account of this.

One night, walking in the grounds of our motel in Palmerston North, Willie John brought me into a discussion he was having with Telfer about line-out blocking. I suggested a method that we had copied from New Zealand on the 1977 tour, which had been successfully adopted by every side I have played for since. It was similar to the one Willie John was recommending to Telfer. The coach agreed to try the method at the following morning's training session, but when we came to it, he had decided against it. There is nothing wrong with single-mindedness, provided the ideas are right. Not that Telfer didn't vary his approach. For instance, before the North Auckland match, he decided on separate meetings for the forwards and backs. He ranted and raved at both – and everything he said must have been overheard, even by the press. I can't imagine what they thought when, in an attempt to gee up Steve Boyle, he said to him: 'Boyley – 19½ stone, if I had a pin I'd pop ye'. Before the third Test, he lined up the forwards in the shower area and in an attempt to provoke our aggression, he went down the line slapping each of the boys across the side of the head. I was at the end of the line and watched in fascination, wondering whether he was going to risk cuffing our biggest player, Maurice Colclough. I could see from Maurice's expression that he wasn't going to have any of it . . . and Telfer didn't try it. Maurice, and the rest of us, got nothing more than a firm tap on the shoulder.

At the end of the tour, Telfer blamed everyone except himself. The players weren't up to standard, he said, and the standards in Britain were way behind the All Blacks. I don't think anyone will argue with the latter view. But Telfer seemed to have forgotten that he was one of those who helped determine those standards. Curiously, when it was all over, Telfer maintained his coaching strategy for the 1983 tour was the right one: as a player, all I can say is that we ended up not knowing what the hell we were doing, because he changed our tactics so many times.

I have been asked many times why Willie John did not intervene. The answer is that the playing side was really nothing to do with him. Probably he did have a quiet word with him once or twice. Only Willie John will be able to say whether Telfer listened or not. I'm sure Telfer would have stood a better chance of producing good tour results had we been able to carry on where we had left off in South Africa in 1980. We had a nucleus of players from that tour who could have developed a pattern and there were enough experienced players who would have been only too pleased to help out on the coaching side. Telfer did not want that.

There also seemed to be a wrong impression that the Lions were up against a gang of thugs, hell-bent on roughing us up in every game. Certainly there were a couple of incidents, notably the stamping of Fitzgerald and the injury to Nigel Melville, which provided raw copy for the reporters. But these were the exceptions rather than the rule. Those of us who know and respect the way New Zealanders play the game, recognise that they have a fundamentally different approach to playing from that in Britain. What may be dirty or dangerous to us, like trampling or raking over bodies in a ruck, is second nature to them, an instinctive part of the hard, forceful way they play. They view the ruck as if the bodies were not on the ground (as in the majority of situations they shouldn't be) and it is the ground they are treading on, not players. If their own players are trodden on in the process, they accept it. In Britain, some of our players tend to squeal about it, or start throwing punches. There are no more dirty players in New Zealand than there are in Britain. The first rule is to accept their approach; the second is to make them aware occasionally that if they go too far retribution will be exacted. There is a lot to be said for the mutual respect achieved in this aspect of the game.

All in all the 1983 tour was a disappointment, certainly for me. I knew it was going to be my last tour, and I would have liked to have gone out on a high note. Even now, I believe we had the potential to win the series. We should have won the first Test and though I knew the All Blacks were a very good side, I fully expected us to improve as much, if not more, than we did. Our team had so much potential and yet it was unfulfilled. That, in the final analysis, was the frustrating aspect of the tour.

Players

As a general rule, players are in the best position to assess the strengths and weaknesses of other players. This is one of the chief reasons why experienced players are sometimes at odds with selectors, and are critical of some of their decisions. This applies to every position on the field, but the selection of prop forwards is particularly fraught with danger. A good example of this is when a prop, who has proved himself supreme in his own country, comes second-best against an opponent from another country, which leads to his being dropped and his place going to someone who is not as good. This does not mean I underestimate the difficulty selectors have in picking the right men for the job. Not everyone agrees about the abilities of individual players, players included, so mistakes are inevitable.

Naturally players are often asked their opinion of opponents – rarely I might add by selectors – and sometimes their opinion causes surprise. I have already stated the high regard in which I hold Fran Cotton, having played with and against the rugged Lancastrian. It is no surprise to me that Fran is on record as rating Robert Paparemborde above me. Fran has not broken the rules of our Mutual Admiration Society in giving his vote to 'Papa' – his evaluation probably being based on the fact that the Frenchman has given him more trouble than I have. The explanation for this lies in both physique and technique. Fran found it less of a problem to play against me simply because I have broad shoulders, which enabled him to gain all-important purchase, whereas Papa, much narrower across the shoulders, was nowhere near as big. He was a curious shape, really, for a prop, with narrow shoulders and broad hips. Cotton probably couldn't get any kind of grip, or position himself so that he could scrummage properly. As regards technique, Papa and I are different again. Cotton found him a very awkward, disruptive opponent because Papa turns in, while my technique is much more orthodox, as I push straight to try and create a platform for everyone in my pack to push on.

Cotton was not alone in finding Papa a troublesome opponent. Colin Smart and Glyn Shaw always had problems with him. To my knowledge only one loose-head, Charlie Faulkner, ever coped comfortably with Papa. Charlie's solution lay in his own immense strength. He was able to force his head under the Frenchman and then bore into the most vulnerable area in the upper body, the side of the rib cage near the floating ribs. Glyn Shaw's failure to counter Papa was more a problem of physique than of technique. Shaw was really a lock forward rather than a prop, but he was not tall enough for the second row and not beefy enough for the front row. Shaw was very strong and possessed a fine physique, but as Ray Prosser would say, he had the right engine but the wrong chassis. His physical limitations were completely exposed by Papa when Wales played France in Paris in 1977, and as a result the Welsh scrummage was in all sorts of trouble. Not only did Papa bore in on Bobby Windsor and split Shaw from him but also the unfortunate Bobby had to contend with the full force and pressure of the tightly bound Alain Paco, the hooker, and Papa. This meant the scrum was disastrously lop-sided.

Our scrummaging was in a mess and I was powerless to do anything about it, or to help Bobby, who was having a terrible time. The situation called for desperate measures, and it didn't take long for me to decide that the only option left was to collapse the scrum. I did this persistently and deliberately throughout the match, and I make no excuse for it, even though I must stress that this was the last occasion when I needed to deliberately bring the scrum down. It is interesting – in view of the current concern over collapsed scrums – that I was not penalised once (Scotland's Alan Hosie was the referee), nor did Cholley or I get hurt in the process. Cholley did suffer a few bruises but a different technique was required for that.

It was understandable that neither Bobby nor I were very impressed with Shaw's contribution to that match, and at the time I questioned both his commitment, and his guts. We expect total support from each other in the front row, and when you don't get it, it is difficult to disguise your contempt for the non-contributor. In retrospect, I may have unfairly maligned Glyn and mistakenly doubted his courage. In his case, the fault lay in his physique and technique, which simply were not good enough. In the end, even the selectors realised the extent of Glyn's limitations. He was never picked again, his place going to Clive Williams, who was infinitely better suited in all respects, and in my view should have won more than ten caps. Clive's misfortune was that he was contemporary at first with Charlie Faulkner, who was in a class of his own at loose-head prop. Charlie's record speaks for itself. He played 19 times for Wales, and was on the losing side in a Championship match only twice – once against Scotland in 1975, once against France in 1979. Certainly it was not due to anything lacking in his contribution that Wales lost twice to Australia and once to New Zealand in 1978.

A footnote to Shaw's exposure by Paparemborde in 1977 was that it denied me the opportunity of squaring accounts with Cholley. I had something to prove, to say the least, against the 6 feet 3 inches, 17 stone Frenchman, known as 'Garth'. Cholley had built up an awesome reputation when I played against him for the first time, at Cardiff Arms Park in 1976. I was told that he was a formidable scrummager, immensely strong and a rugged, uncompromising character in everything else he did. I discovered in the first scrum, that Cholley's reputation was in no way exaggerated: he clawed at my face with such ferocity that I had no choice but to retaliate. With both arms otherwise engaged, my only weapon was my teeth so I sank them into his thumb. Cholley squealed like a stuck pig and, incredibly, complained to the referee, John West, about this insult to his manhood. John West's eyesight has been the cause of some speculation on other occasions; this time he walked over to Bobby Windsor and lectured him for the misdemeanour.

Bobby's incredulous innocence was quite something to behold.

Cholley, momentarily, accepted he would be more usefully employed at loose-head, and I was quite enjoying our particular contest, even finding time to peel from a line-out and set up a ruck from which Steve Fenwick cleverly manoeuvered a try for J. J. Williams. 'Garth', though, is the unforgiving sort and half an hour later, he found another opportunity to practise his particular brand of facial massage. This time it was out in the open. I was trying to set up a ruck and was isolated, sandwiched by Palmié and Imbernon. Cholley came in behind us, his claws this time raking at my eyes. The result was a scratched cornea, and I had to go off the field for the first time in my international career. My misfortune provided a memorable moment for someone else. Mike Knill, of Cardiff, came on to replace me and win his only cap. This had an amusing sequel. Mike's wife, Jan, came up to me afterwards, tearfully and apologetically explaining that although she had for weeks been sticking pins into my effigy, she really didn't intend that I should come to any serious harm. 'I didn't mean it, Graham, honest' Jan said, 'I only wanted you to catch a cold or something so that Mike could get his cap.'

Unfortunately, I didn't have many opportunities to redress the balance with Cholley, as I played against him on two other occasions only. I believe that he could have been a first-class prop, had he concentrated his efforts in that direction. Given his strength and weight, he was without doubt built for the job.

When I look back over the years, and try to assess my opposite numbers, Cholley inevitably comes top of the list. Certainly he was the most difficult opponent I have played against, and the strongest. I have come up against bigger men – for example Flippie van der Merwe, of Western Province, whose 297 pounds (over 21 stone) I came face to face with when playing for the Lions against a South African Invitation XV at Olen Park, Potchefstroom on 21 May 1980. In comparison, Cholley outweighed me by more than two stone. As the Frenchman's chief asset was his great strength, it is hardly surprising he didn't have to rely on technique to get the better of an opponent. With Cholley there was no slipping out or turning inwards in order to relieve the pressure or perhaps to put his opponent in a weaker position. Cholley would take you full on, in an effort to force you to the limits of your endurance. It was sheer aggression from first scrum to last. The problem was that Cholley would not leave it at that; intimidation for 80 minutes was usually the order of the day. I have already described his technique at our first meeting, in 1976. A year later, the intimidation began before kick-off at Parc des Princes. As we lined-up ready for France to kick off, I saw Cholley point at the ground with one hand and wave the other in a clenched fist. It occurred to me that the message he was trying to get across was what might happen to me if I collapsed any scrum.

In the event, the Welsh scrum was under pressure immediately, because in the selectors' search for greater mobility, Charlie Faulkner had been dropped in favour of Glyn Shaw at loose-head. When I say pressure, I mean pressure: Bobby Windsor had to hook with his head and I was forced to collapse almost every scrum on our put-in. In order to prevent the inevitable booting, I made sure Cholley was my cushion. I manoeuvered him between Palmié and myself at every opportunity. What seemed lost on Cholley was the fact that his sttength was his most powerful weapon; it would have been of the greatest concern for most international-class props. Personally I would worry more about my opponent's ability than about taking a good booting. I would prefer to take a few clouts, rather than be pushed backwards.

Cholley's reputation as a rough-neck is hardly surprising. His introduction to rugby was unusual, to say the least. The story goes that he and some fellow French paratroopers were involved in a long drawn-out brawl in a bar which was owned apparently by the president of the Castres club. At the end of the punch-up Cholley was the only man left standing, which so impressed the Castres official that he decided then and there that Cholley had to be bought out of the paratroopers so that he could play for Castres.

Talking of punch-ups inevitably turns my mind to the Steve Finnane incident in Australia 1978. I hasten to say that I do not connect Cholley with Finnane in any way. That would be insulting to Cholley, who was a good prop. Finnane was branded a thug throughout the rugby world after he broke my jaw in two places with a punch from behind in the second Test at Sydney. My only comment is that he was, by far, the poorest prop I ever played against in an international. When I returned to Australia in April 1981 to play in the World Barbarians team against Sydney, a few local reporters felt duty bound to rake through the ashes of the controversy. Did I hold any grudges against Finnane? Had the incident affected my opinion of Australia or Australian rugby? The questions were clearly loaded. My response was polite and guarded: it was just one of those things, I declared. Certainly I had no wish to stir things up, particularly on an occasion which was intended as a celebration.

Finnane did have the opportunity to explain his part in the affair, and to apologise if he thought necessary, in his book. 'I only wish' he wrote, 'it had done no more than I intended it to do – to show Price and the other Welshmen that Australians would not bow to standover tactics.' Whether he intended ambiguity, I do not know. But to me it was an eloquent testimony of the character of a man, who, not being a very good player, sought vindication behind feeble chauvinism. Frankly, my recollection is understandably hazy since I neither expected a punch nor, with my back to Finnane, knew where it came from until I went down. So the instinctive reaction which often lessens the effect of a punch was absent; and was probably the reason why the injury was so severe. In the event, my jaw had to be wired up and I had to wear a curious protective frame for over two months. Much of the credit for the success of the operation must go to my dentist, John Evans, who made the arrangements, and to the surgeon, Mr Gibson, and his excellent staff at St Lawrence's Hospital, Chepstow, who put the pieces back in the right places. I took a lot of ribbing when I ventured out again in public, for I must have looked a little like a refugee from an astronauts' training camp. 'Desperate Dan' was one of my more flattering nicknames; what mattered most though was that I was soon as good as new, indeed I am convinced my chin is now stronger than ever. However, I'm not inviting anyone to prove it, Finnane included!

Scotland's Mighty Mouse, Ian McLauchlan, was technically the best prop I have played against, but the best all-round prop I have faced was Fran Cotton. Fran could play on either head with equal ease and without becoming less efficient. I think, though, he was better at loose-head. Although nowhere near as powerful as Cholley, Fran was strong enough to do a very good job. He was also very fit and consequently he was able to make an effective contribution at rucks and mauls (instead, as a lot of props tend to do, get there only for a rest or too late to affect the outcome). He was also capable of expanding his game by being involved in loose play. On the 1977 Lions tour to New Zealand, Fran used to be the first man around on the peel; and he was quite prepared to set up the play for the rest of us, whereas many props would take the opportunity of making ground themselves. He would commit the opposition back row, which enabled his supporting forwards to drive through into the clear. A classic example of this was Fran's part in the play which led up to Dougie Morgan's try against the All Blacks in the fourth Test at Eden Park, Auckland.

I've already said that I considered Clive Williams, of Swansea, to be an underrated loose-head prop. Clive invariably gave me a difficult game, particularly in the early stages of my career. He always asked me to consider all sorts of questions of technique and commitment. As decent a player as he is a man, Clive was a completely honest scrummager, who would never shirk the hard work, even if it meant that he could have avoided taking a hiding himself. When he played for Wales, Clive gave everything. The shabby way he was cast aside in 1983 was outrageous.

While discussing loose-head props, it would be impossible to omit Charlie Faulkner. Although I never played against him –

thank goodness – he ranked among the best, because some of the tight-head props I respect most have told me so. Charlie was limited in that he was not exactly the quickest man on the paddock, but curiously it was never noticeable in a match. Certainly he was fast enough to score a notable try against Ireland and I lost count of the number of occasions when he was up in support when the wing was scoring in the corner. Charlie's strength and commitment as a scrummager were his greatest assets.

Another prop whom I never confronted directly in the scrummage was Paparemborde. He was obviously very good. You could always feel the effect on my side of the scrum of his influence on the other side! His unorthodox technique troubled many loose-heads. In boxing terms I suppose he would have been equivalent to a Southpaw. Against Wales Papa would attempt to unsettle the hooker by twisting in and downwards. Often I could feel the scrum crab sideways once Papa had 'engaged' and the French applied pressure. He was also an accomplished player in the loose, and a notable try scorer in internationals. He was also one of the cleanest French forwards I have played against; his ability and technique were far more effective than a punch or a boot.

Papa spoke good English too. During the Western Province centenary matches in South Africa in 1983, Papa seemed likely to come in for a little bit of leather on one occasion from one particularly rough South African forward, Murray Dawson, the Natal loose-head prop. John Perkins, my Pontypool club-mate, was playing in the same team as Papa, recognised the threat and decided to intervene to save his colleague. The result was that Perky took Dawson's punches, and ended up with a broken nose and two black eyes. Papa was obviously very grateful for the timely intervention. He came up to the dazed Perky, patted him on the back and said: 'Tzank you, Per-kee, Tzank you'.

Laws and Referees

The new binding Law was introduced, I suppose, because of the dangers of collapsed scrummages, legislation coming after numerous warnings that one day a player would break his neck or suffer some permanent damage when a scrum collapsed. Without any knowledge of the number of injuries sustained on the rugby field, well-meaning folk caused the administrators to have nightmarish visions of a traffic jam of wheelchairs containing props and hookers. You can be hurt, of course, when a scrum collapses as indeed you can be injured in a ruck, maul or a tackle. Personally, I know of only a few who have been seriously hurt because of a collapsed scrum, whereas the history of the game is sprinkled with incidents of terrible injuries suffered in, for example, a tackle or a ruck.

However, there has been no outcry against that kind of risk, or any legislation to prevent it. What have been overlooked by our no doubt well-meaning Lawmakers, are the measures rugby players take to insure themselves against injury, a 'survival' policy which applies just as much to front-row men in a collapsed scrum as it does to a player caught beneath the flashing boots in a ruck. Every player in the front row knows when a scrum is deliberately collapsed, and takes appropriate safeguards. Like a good wrestler, you learn how to fall. The problem is not the deliberate collapsed scrum, but the accidental one, which happens far more often. Caught unawares, the players are at risk – but how on earth can you legislate against an accident? If you take the argument to its logical conclusion, the Lawmakers might as well say: 'we'll allow you to deliberately collapse a scrum, but we will stop you accidentally collapsing one.' Obviously, that would be absurd but I believe it underlines the lack of thought – and lack of consultation with the front-line troops – which seems to accompany most new legislation in the game.

The new binding Law was a prime example of a little-considered piece of rugby legislation. I'm told, on fairly good authority, that the new technique was 'tested' by two members of the International Board in some bar during a break in their meeting. They scrummed down against each other, experimenting with arm positions like ticktack men before finally announcing: 'that's it, it works'. The story may be questionable but if it is remotely true then we players can tremble only with alarm. Fortunately, the game has evolved in such a way as to have developed safeguards against thoughtless, naïve legislation. The new binding Law was fully tested, this time by experienced, current players, at a coaching session run by the Welsh Rugby Union at Aberystwyth. It was not only found to be unworkable, but contrary to its purpose, contained an element of risk far more tangible and worrying than that which prompted the Law's introduction in the first place. As a result of this realistic test, the WRU sensibly ordered that the new Law should be ignored in matches played in Wales.

I find the phobia about collapsed scrums baffling. They seldom happen today, and the legislation came in long after players themselves had changed their techniques, and their attitude to collapsed scrums. Not only was the Law outdated, but so were the referees. In fact, many referees do not have a clue why a scrum collapses, what the cause was, or who was responsible. For example, how many of them realise that the back row are often to blame when the scrum goes down? Without wishing to be too technical, a scrum is about weights and balances, thrusts and concessions. It is a delicate balance and it does not take much to upset it. A wet, greasy pitch can be a factor, because of loss of footing or if, for instance, near their own line a nervous back row stop scrummaging and get up ready to 'fly', the equilibrium goes and down drops the scrum. What do referees do? They penalise the front row, which is ridiculous. If, for example, I am packing really low at the moment the back row disengages, there is absolutely nothing I can do to stop the front row from going down in a heap. To be penalised in these circumstances makes you angry and also underlines just how ignorant referees can be.

A case in point was in Wales's match against the Maoris in 1982. Twice their back-row men disengaged, which meant they had less weight in the pack and our scrummage went forward and down. Nothing on earth could have prevented the collapses. However, the referee, Alan Welsby, of England, ignored one collapse and penalised me as the cause of the other. We even had an inquest over it, at the next Welsh squad session, conducted by John Bevan, our coach. To this day, even Bevan believes I was to blame. Take yet another example, when Terry Holmes scored against Ireland at Cardiff in 1983. We had a scrummage on their line, and everyone knew exactly what Holmes was going to do. As a result, Fergus Slattery disengaged to prepare himself for Holmes' burst for the line. No one stopped Holmes from a couple of yards out, but what happened to the scrum? It was all in a heap behind him, simply because the Irish pack could no longer hold our weight. Was that anyone's fault? Of course not.

I remember too the Lions pack being driven backwards by the All Blacks in the Second Test at Wellington in the summer of 1983. Our back row flew, the All Blacks held the ball and then simply drove. There was no collapse. They just drove forward and we could not hold them. Personally, I believe I have been unfairly blamed for collapsed scrums on many occasions. The referees, I suppose, felt secure in singling me out, because they knew their decision could not be questioned from the stand. At one stage in my career it was so bad, that I believe that if the North Stand at the Arms Park had collapsed, I would have been blamed for it. As I have already admitted, there was a time when I deliberately collapsed scrums. In those days, you actually received a certain amount of credit for it, because it meant that you had got the better of your opposing prop. Now, if you do exactly the same thing, you are considered to have had a bad match.

Referees, even the top ones, are in a dilemma over the whole question of collapsed scrums. I have talked to many of them and they all have different ideas as to what happens. What it means, of course, is that while some may be right others are bound to be wrong. Some are completely confused, and have admitted on the field: 'I don't know who is responsible for collapsing the scrum, but I am going to penalise alternately until it stops.' Some referees take their job very seriously, and are eager to learn. They will talk to the players afterwards, and listen to the explanations. Others are either too proud or are convinced they know it all. One referee, I think, who has got it wrong is Clive Norling, of Wales, who is supposed to be one of the best referees in the world. He has simplified the whole matter: if the tight-head prop has his feet positioned backwards, he will not hold him responsible. If the prop has his feet placed forward, however, then Norling will suspect that he is to blame for a collapse. Such judgement ignores one basic element of scrummaging. If a prop has his feet forward, it means not only that he is taking twice as much weight on his legs, but by inference he is positioning himself to prevent the scrum collapsing. Much depends on whom I am scrummaging against, but generally a prop alters his feet position or his scrummaging height as part of his job. It is not to deliberately drop a scrum. At one time, up to, say, 1977, it was a generally accepted ploy to deliberately collapse a scrum to protect your own possession and prevent your scrum being pushed back. It was the easiest way to obtain clean scrummage ball. Was is the operative word. It no longer applies. No one does it any more. The trouble is that referees don't realise that a fundamental change in scrummaging technique has taken place. They, and the Lawmakers, are behind the times.

Norling, incidentally, is the only referee I know who, quite rightly, doubts the legality of wheeling a scrum. According to the Lawbook, the scrummage push must be exerted in a forward direction. A wheeled scrum, however, requires the tight-head prop to stop pushing and actually pull his opposite number rather than push which, of course, means the technique of wheeling is illegal. There is nothing that the opposing front row can do to stop the wheel. Norling actually awarded a penalty against a side which employed the wheel in a match I was playing in – and no one on the field or watching in the stands knew what the offence was for.

Roger Quittenton is not a highly regarded referee, particularly in Wales, mainly because of his misjudgement in giving New Zealand a late match-winning penalty at Cardiff in 1978. That incident should haunt Quittenton for the rest of his life. He has defended his decision, but I'm sure he knows in his heart he made a mistake. I hope one day he decides to write a book; it would provide him with the opportunity to express his regrets. Indeed, I believe he would gain much respect and praise if he admitted he was wrong. It will not affect the result, of course. It was a win for New Zealand, and nothing will change that. What it would do is to wipe the slate clean as far as Geoff Wheel is concerned, and the whole affair would eventually go down as just one of those things. I feel strongly on the matter because I know Geoff was innocent, or at least his so-called offence did not merit a penalty award. I know that because I stood only a few feet from Wheel in the fatal line-out, much closer than Quittenton, and had a clear view of events. For 79 minutes the referee had virtually ignored the line-out: both sides indulged in barging, climbing, lifting and interference and Quittenton allowed it to happen. With Wales 12–10 in front the All Blacks were desperate, and they really were clutching at straws in that last line-out when Andy Haden and Frank Oliver dived out so dramatically. It was so unsubtle as to be unbelievable; the only trouble was Quittenton, I'm convinced, did believe that Haden and Oliver had been unceremoniously barged. It is also possible that later instead of being prepared to admit that he had been taken in, he decided instead to say the penalty was for something else.

One should not overlook another factor; in penalising Wales with a minute to go, he committed the cardinal sin of referees in international matches. They have an unwritten law that they will not award a penalty in a close match in the final few minutes unless the offence is of a highly serious or blatant nature. Wheel's 'offence' hardly came into either category. If anything he was more sinned against than actually sinning: the wily Oliver had deliberately backed into him before plunging away in the grand manner. All Wheel did was to fend him off using his inside arm. I believe it was significant that Quittenton later alleged he had not penalised the 'dives', and that he had awarded the penalty against Wheel for employing a lift on Oliver's shoulder. This confirms that the referee witnessed the dives by the New Zealanders, and makes it most odd that he should have ignored these penalty-seeking acts of transgression, preferring to punish an insignificant infringement. Both Haden and Oliver should have been penalised, as the referee knows, under the law concerning misconduct. That alone should have overruled any decision he might have made in the heat of the moment regarding Wheel. Had he penalised Haden and Oliver, the New Zealanders would not have been surprised. As it was, they could hardly believe their luck that their last-ditch piece of trickery had worked. Brian McKecknie's penalty flew straight to its mark and New Zealand had won.

Quittenton's subsequent explanation of the incident was put into perspective by the reaction of Ian Eliason who watched the dives live on television in New Zealand. The Taranaki lock, who was a popular tourist to Britain with the 1972 All Blacks, was reported to have cried indignantly: 'They've stolen my trick, they've stolen my trick'! Haden, Oliver and Mourie, the captain, have since admitted their part in the gamble to get the penalty. Personally, all I say is good luck to them for trying it – and getting away with it. It won the All Blacks the match, and therefore the end justified the means. But I'm sure that had Quittenton been much more strict in the line-out earlier in the match, I don't think they'd have even attempted something so obvious. How those All Black forwards stopped themselves from falling over with laughter when the referee was taken in, I'll never know . . . .

Roger Quittenton and I have not seen eye-to-eye on other

occasions. When Pontypool played Australia in 1981, Quittenton changed the whole course of the match because he wrongly interpreted what was happening in the scrum. Early in the match, we pushed them off the ball in a couple of scrums and were in the process of repeating it in the third scrum. This time we heaved their front row right over their second row, with the result that the scrum collapsed. Quittenton, amazingly, held us responsible for the collapse, even though it was their put-in and it would have obviously been to Pontypool's disadvantage for the scrum to collapse. We were penalised, Australia kicked the goal, and afraid that Quittenton might repeat the punishment, we had to change our whole approach and technique. I believe it was a major factor in losing us the match.

A few weeks before that, Quittenton was the referee when Pontypool played Gloucester at Kingsholm, which is a ground where props earn and lose their stripes. In other words, like Pontypool, Gloucester have a tradition in forward play and scrummaging. There is no pussy-footing, either way, when you play against Gloucester. On this occasion, I was propping against a youngster called Malcolm Preedy, who was thought highly enough of to tour with England in the USA. Preedy was prominent about the field, but at that time he didn't have the strength or technique to pose a real threat in the scrums. We drove them back regularly and Preedy tended to give way under pressure. Perhaps naïvely, I thought Preedy was learning some of the facts of life of prop-forward play. Roger Quittenton considered otherwise. After one scrum had gone down, he made a point of calling me aside. For a moment, I thought he was going to send me off. The essence of our 'chat', however, was that Quittenton wanted me to take it easy on Preedy, that I should not scrummage so hard because Preedy was only a youngster and was obviously not strong enough to hold up the scrum. To say I was incredulous, is an understatement. When I think that this took place at Kingsholm, I almost believe it didn't happen at all. A few Gloucester props will never believe it, I know.

If there is one lesson I have learned during my long association with rugby, it is not to be surprised by what referees do. Corris Thomas is a case in point. Corris, who left the game recently because he said he was no longer enjoying it, was one of those referees with a reputation for trying to keep a match flowing. That philosophy appeals to spectators and to clubs only too grateful for a referee who will overlook their errors. It certainly does not appeal to a club like Pontypool, whose game is based on forcing others into mistakes and then punishing those mistakes with penalties. Corris Thomas's approach did not take this into consideration when we played Newbridge in the quarter-final of the Welsh Cup in 1982. Brendan McAloon gave Newbridge an early lead with a penalty goal, but from then on we were encamped on or near their 25. We put tremendous pressure on them through our forwards, and they were forced to defend desperately. That we failed to score half-a-dozen tries was our fault: that Newbridge's defence was excellent was to their credit. My complaint is that the referee never once saw fit to award us a single penalty for offside or for killing the ball in rucks, which Newbridge, who were not a disciplined side, resorted to frequently. We lost 0–3. A few days earlier, with a different referee, we had beaten them comfortably. A few weeks later, with yet another referee, and with a much weakened side, we defeated them again. In each case, penalties were abundantly ordered and were kicked.

The players, who are most affected by Law changes, are understandably often suspicious of the motives for some alterations. It is inexplicable that players are never consulted and that they are not asked their views. We are told, for example, about the 'concern' – whose concern, players or administrators? – over the line-out generally and the specific problem caused when the jumper leans on an opponent with his inside arm when making a tap-back with the other. Of course, the fur flies when it happens, retaliation usually being the only choice because referees either turn a blind eye to it or do not see it. The solution seems to me so simple, it is amazing that even our Lawmakers have not thought of it: all that is needed is a Law which orders that the jumper must only use his inside arm, or both arms, when going for a tap ball. There would be no leaning on, and no repercussions. That it might also improve the quality of possession from a line-out would be an added bonus. The main advantage would be the elimination of one of those flash-point situations, which believe me, players are only too anxious to avoid.

I hope none of the foregoing suggests I have no sympathy with the task that faces referees, because I do. Sometimes their job borders on the impossible. Take, for instance, the scrummage. I am told that one referee – I believe it was Johnny Johnston, of England – actually sat down and tried to analyse how many offences were possible in a scrum. I think he found there were 144, which is in itself a convincing argument for a total rethink on the Laws generally.

The Laws of rugby football, as presently framed, are a mess. Ambiguity is the biggest evil, and most of the problems from a playing point of view stem from this. The International Board, the Lawmakers and governors of the game, seemed aware of this when they decided several years ago that a rewrite of the Laws was essential. It is tragic that they have abandoned the project. The complexity of the current Laws and the way they are interpreted in different countries is the biggest problem in the game. Indeed, I have no doubt rugby football has reached crisis point for with the game expanding world-wide, the way it is played is more important than ever. And the way the game is played is decided, not by coaches or coaching, but by the Laws themselves. If the Laws are bad, the game is bad. A bad game implies a lack of enjoyment and satisfaction in both player and spectator. The consequences of any further lowering of morale in this respect could be disastrous, including the very real danger of a breakaway by some countries, dissatisfied with the absence of firm government. The IB's competence to run the game has never been so openly questioned. The possibility, too, of a professional tournament still looms large and it would be foolish to ignore. The threat of a breakaway or a professional alternative would not be in the loss of top players, which even our badly directed game could shrug off, but in the type of game the rebels would create. Without doubt, their first act would be to abandon the present rulebook and draft new rules. It does not necessarily follow that new rules and a new game would be more appealing to players and spectators. But the chance that it would be is a chance rugby football must not take.

Not all new rugby legislation is detrimental. The adoption of the Australian Dispensation Rule, which allows direct kicking to touch from inside the kickers' 22-metre line only, and the decision not to describe a fumble as a knock-on, were enormously beneficial to the game. So too was the introduction of replacements. The only disappointment is that all three took so long to introduce as they should have been part of the game many, many years ago.

The present Laws have taken over a 100 years to evolve, so it would be unrealistic to expect them to be redrafted overnight. While that must be the long term objective, I believe an interim compromise is practical and desirable. The men to do this are the world's top referees who, as a first basic step, should be commissioned to get together not necessarily to rewrite the Laws but to establish uniform interpretation. Inconsistency in interpretation of the Laws has reached unacceptable levels: today's player is totally confused, not knowing what is expected of him, not only in different countries, but often in his own country and from match to match. Get rid of inconsistency and you have taken the first positive step to improving the game everywhere, and restoring players' faith and enjoyment, which have diminished alarmingly in recent years. If referees are to be given such a wide-ranging brief, naturally you would expect them to co-opt anyone that they felt could help them in their task. I'm sure senior, experienced players would jump at the chance.

Whenever players get together to discuss respective Laws or Law changes, they generally agree on one thing: that the Laws are made and altered by the wrong people, largely because their knowledge of the playing side is out-of-date. The game they played is light years away from today's game. The modern player is better coached, he is probably more skilled, he is much fitter and faster, and technically he is more correct. It follows that contemporary players have a far greater knowledge and understanding than past players, who played an altogether different game. Not to take advantage of that knowledge, not to consult players and coaches is one of the many weaknesses in the system of Law-making.

There are plenty of examples where players might have been able to help. Take for instance the tackle Law. Originally a player was allowed to pass even though he was tackled, provided the ball did not touch the ground. The intent was to speed up the game, to make it more fluid. The side-effect, however, was the pile-up. Oh, horror, said the Lawmakers, we've got to stop that. Having decided what the problem was, rather than the cause, they outlawed both the pass from a tackle and thus the pile-up – a completely retrograde step. A more beneficial approach would have been to reassess the meaning of a tackle, deciding perhaps that a player is not tackled unless the ball touches the ground. Either tackler or tackled player must play the ball by passing it or placing the ball in a position of advantage to his own side. If the player, for any reason, is unable to play the ball in such a way, he must not restrict someone else from playing it. If a third player or more becomes involved, the rule should be that he must be on his feet to play the ball.

The interpretation of rucking is a bone of contention throughout the world. In my view, the only country which employs the ruck properly and according to Law is New Zealand. Technically, a ruck is driving over the ball on the ground by players binding together, forming a loose type of scrummage, and using the head and shoulders as a kind of battering ram. The technique is the easy part and in theory the side with the better technique comes off best. But what happens when there are bodies lying on the ground? New Zealand referees have no doubts as to interpretation. They will allow the stepping on of players, of either side, if a ruck is in progress. It is acceptable by all – referees, players, press and spectators.

In Britain, however, it is totally unacceptable and players

here often are penalised for trampling. Ironically, the only time we can 'get away with it' in Britain, is if all eight forwards drive onward in unison, regardless of the kicking, stamping or raking that might be involved. If a solitary player tries the same thing, he risks being sent off. What this means is that British sides are generally prevented from employing or perfecting an absolutely legitimate tactic. The best rucking inevitably leads to treading on bodies. To avoid a player on the ground means you either have to change your stride or make a deft side-step; with several players on the ground such dexterity is nearly impossible, unless one adopts a less efficient rucking technique. As a result, the less competent side in rucking gains an undeserved advantage. The ruck remains one of the most frustrating aspects of the British game. As I keep telling my New Zealand pals, it's not that we can't execute a ruck, we are simply not allowed to. When you consider the importance of the ruck in All Blacks play, it is little wonder that British Lions sides are at a disadvantage.

According to the rulebook, a player is offside from a kick ahead by one of his own team only if he is within 10 metres of the opponent fielding the kick. In Britain, we tend to hang back, to allow the kicker to follow up and by running past, put us all on-side. The Australians interpreted the Law rather differently, as Wales found out to their cost on their 1978 tour. The Australians, in fact, made life very difficult for us by the simple procedure of kicking the ball long down the middle of the field and every one of them chasing like mad, preserving their on-side status when 10 metres from the Welsh player who had fielded the kick. Inevitably those close to the off-side point were put on-side when the fielder ran 5 metres, which happened a great deal because we tried to counterattack from deep positions. With so many Australian players up, however, such counterattacks proved difficult to execute and we were often put under tremendous pressure because of it. In Britain, it would have been different. There would not have been so many players up, and counterattacking would have been more practical. Regardless of other factors, I believe the Australian method – which was correct by the rules – was a major reason why we lost four matches, including both Tests.

One last comment on referees. Is it not strange that so few of them have had the advantage of going through the grades as a player? That none of the top ones have ever played international rugby, and only a handful have ever played first-class rugby? I have no doubt that they all know the rulebook inside out and can quote it verbatim, but are they really sympathetic and appreciative of the players' point of view?

To be fair to referees, their job is a difficult one: they are expected to have eyes in the back of their heads and because of the complexity of their job it is impossible for them to please everyone all the time. At the same time, they must accept justifiable criticism, which is an occupational hazard of any job. As the sole judges of events on the field they are invested with enormous responsibility. In my view, the referees' most important responsibility is the maintenance of discipline. It is generally acknowledged that the way to do this is by gaining the respect of the players, by indicating, for example, that they are prepared to send anyone off for foul play. Let us have no argument on this score. A blatant, premeditated foul merits an early bath, and the game has developed stringent punishments for offenders.

At the same time, it is not so readily appreciated or understood that most acts of foul play are the result of frustration on the part of the offender, and retaliation by the player who becomes the object of that frustration. Players don't just happen to become frustrated: nine times out of ten the cause is the referee's inability to control certain aspects of a match. The ruck and line-out are prime examples.

In the line-out, obstruction, barging, impeding, or holding down a jumper are the principal causes of players' frustration. Some players can contain it, others appeal to the referee, while others, their tolerance limit passed, lash out. This results in a penalty and perhaps a sending-off and a suspension. Yet for the trained eye, all these causes are obvious: you do not have to be eagle-eyed to spot a jumper going for the ball with his outside arm and using his inside arm to hold down his opposite number. Something must also be wrong when, say, a tall, athletic line-out technician with a reputation for winning the ball cleanly, loses out to a shorter, heavier player who looks as if he would have difficulty jumping over a matchbox. Referees often opt out of their responsibilities in both respects. Where does this leave the offended player? His reputation for ball winning might be questioned, his place in the side might even be jeopardised. His reaction is therefore understandable.

In the case of rucks, a side trying to ruck in, say, the style of the All Blacks, can be thwarted by a pack who haven't an ounce of conventional ball winning skill, but who kill the ball and turn rucks into pile-ups in which there is no offside and handling of the ball is allowed to the player on the ground. In this instance, referees do not help by failing to immediately penalise for killing the ball. If such offenders were instantly punished, they would soon realise that they were not going to get away with similar offences. The rucking side would then be able to perform their function properly, for it follows that the cause of the pile-up is no longer a problem. Ray Prosser, incidentally, has a golden rule about rucks. The last man to arrive at the ruck must never tread on a body, as after, say, the first seven forwards have driven through, the last man will possibly be the only one to attract the referee's notice and might be liable to be penalised.

These are only two particular instances when referees' control is vital. There are others, of course. But in general, the amount of violence would be greatly reduced, if referees penalised the instigators and not the players who react against these unfair practices. It goes without saying, that this would result in players with real ability being allowed to do themselves justice.

Justice concerns us all, particularly regarding the punishment for offences committed on the field. Unlike a court of law, where you are innocent until proved guilty, a player (at least in Wales) is considered guilty from the moment he is sent off. He will automatically be suspended, but as the circumstances of his offence are not discussed, this suspension is predetermined. Only the extent of his guilt is considered at the disciplinary hearing. It cannot be right that a half-hearted reaction, say, in self defence, merits the same four-week suspension as a premeditated punch from behind. Nor does it make sense that an offence such as treading on bodies in a ruck (which is acceptable to most referees) be punished by the same six-week suspension that follows a deliberate kick in the head.

It is disappointing that a player is not given the chance to prove his innocence or at least to plead mitigating circumstances or appeal against the severity of his sentence. I have known of players being sent off, when a reprimand would have been sufficient. There have been cases, too, in which players have been accused of acts of foul play which were physically impossible to commit. Yet these players were found guilty without trial, their cases not considered by a jury but by a sentencing committee. The point is that referees, like everyone else, are not infallible. They make mistakes, which is understandable when their decisions to send someone off are often made in the heat of a moment. Once that player is off the field, he is suspended which cannot be right. The only automatic element at disciplinary meetings should be a player's right to be represented. He should be allowed to present his case, his evidence being produced if not to prove his innocence, at least to try to obtain a fair sentence.

When Gareth John, of Swansea, and Paul Koteka, the Maoris' prop, were sent off during the Swansea–Maoris match in 1982, they were given short three-match suspensions. This was entirely due to the fact that the disciplinary committee which heard the case included the Maori manager, Waka Nathan. The case caused quite a stir particularly in Wales, because at the time players from other clubs had been given much more severe sentences for comparatively less serious offences. I think that the whole disciplinary procedure should be overhauled. It is absurd that the punishment should be given before the crime has been established.

The Future

During the 20 years I have been playing rugby football, much of that time at high level, it has probably been one of the most significant eras in the history of the game. Rugby has undergone some remarkable changes in my lifetime, developing from a relatively minor sport into a world-wide one. And I believe that it will – and must – change even more in the next few years if the progress is to continue at the same rate.

The idea of rugby as a genuinely amateur sport is as old and dead as those who pioneered it. I am not suggesting rugby football should become totally professional, but as in the case of other major sports which started off as completely amateur, there is a need to introduce a professional element. All the sports that have gone over such as athletics, football, golf, lawn tennis, cricket, and squash have developed a two-tier structure, professional at the top and amateur at the bottom. All exist side by side in a happy, acceptable compromise.

The only question is not whether rugby football should follow suit, but to what extent it can afford to introduce professionalism at the higher level. Rugby football is undoubtedly a wealthy, influential game. It has become too big a money-spinner for it to remain totally amateur. International matches in both the southern and northern hemispheres attract large crowds and revenue is supplemented by vast and increasing television coverage. This income runs into not thousands but millions of pounds. The cost of major tours, for instance, is usually recouped after a few matches only; the rest is sheer profit flowing into the coffers of the respective rugby unions.

True, this money is used to develop the game, and the huge, impressive edifices throughout the major rugby-playing countries are evidence of this. The stadiums in New Zealand, South Africa, Wales, France, Scotland, Ireland and England are magnificent. Most are freehold, valuable properties, which are the envy of many other sports. Most major countries have professional administrators too, who are an inevitable consequence of the money element within the game. Rugby football has become a business and a big one at that. The only people in the game who are not benefiting from rugby's success are its most important component – the players. I am not for one moment suggesting that leading rugby players should be treated similarly to £1000 a week footballers. Rich though the game is, there is insufficient money at club level for a player to earn his living from playing.

I think rugby needs a semi-professional approach, with players at the top level benefiting from the income that their presence on the field brings in. It would make life so much more attractive and comfortable, and in some ways would help justify the enormous sacrifices that top-class players have to make to attain their level of skill and fitness. The standard riposte from those who want to maintain the status quo is: 'It was your choice to play the game. You must accept the rules.' Yet there is no valid reason for keeping rugby fully amateur or in maintaining the so-called 'amateur spirit'. Rugby is not a better game because players are amateur. It would probably be a better game and far more enjoyable for the players if there were some positive rewards. After all my years in the game, it seems to me that the only people who actually believe in a totally amateur concept are those that can afford to and they are most definitely not the players.

The honour of playing for one's country is one thing. But unfortunately honour doesn't pay the mortgage, nor does it feed and clothe the family. Rugby players, like their counterparts in other sports, are entertainers, and should be treated accordingly. I think a player should be allowed to benefit from his popularity – advertising products, after dinner speaking, endorsing equipment and gear. Yes, even writing a book! I'm sure that a mutually beneficial arrangement could be arrived at in which the leading players would be allowed to reap some of the rewards of their success and, for instance, put a percentage of their earnings back into the game. The situation as it now stands is ludicrous. Because of its antiquated Laws, the game loses many of its leading players with all their valuable experience and knowledge because for one reason or another they break the amateur code. The game cannot afford this migration.

What is an amateur anyway? Strictly speaking, players are already professional. The moment they accept, say, expenses for a Lions tour they become professionalised. When their employers, too, pay them for their leave of absence, is that not being paid for playing? Of course it is. It wouldn't really take very much to end this hypocritical situation and make everything legal and above board. Ever since the game started, there have been 'backhanders' of sorts. The only trouble is that usually everything has been kept quiet. The 'presents' from clubs, the topping up of expenses, transfer fees and the like have been under the counter. The great unmentionables.

One particular club treasurer recently resigned because a new player, and a good one at that, was paid £1000 'signing-on' fee. He wasn't arguing about the payment, merely the size of it! Or in contrast, the wage war that exists when small, local clubs vie for players. 'What are they paying you? £5? Right, we'll make it £6.' The law of supply and demand is no different in rugby football than it is in business. And don't get the idea that this sort of thing happens only in Wales. It is rife in many countries, particularly France. I know of one senior English club at least, which offers inducements to players. These take various forms, sometimes a job, sometimes a job and accommodation. Occasionally it is a job, accommodation, free air fare and expenses. It is not breaking the rules, of course, merely bending them.

I am not sure what Andy Haden thought about the rules. He has probably not even read them! He seems to have found a way around the amateur regulations, clearly to the embarrassment of the NZRFU. If Haden were not such a tremendous player, I doubt whether he would have got away with it. But while still playing for the All Blacks, he writes a regular column in a Sunday newspaper for which he is paid, and yet still retains his amateur status. He wrote a book too, declaring he would accept payment for it. In contrast, Graham Mourie wrote a book, declared his intention to be paid, and lost his amateur status. It was the same with Fran Cotton, Gareth Edwards, Phil Bennett and Bill Beaumont. The game has now lost those players. It is absurd. The players' frustration is increased when they see the financial wheelings and dealings of their respective unions. While they discuss sponsorship deals in large figures, or they employ marketing firms to raise revenue, they not only frown on much smaller negotiations but impose bans on them as if the person involved has broken one of the Ten Commandments.

Let me give a few personal examples. After I broke my jaw in Australia, I was unable to eat properly. All my food had to be liquidised, even including fish and chips! That I drank and enjoyed milk soon came to the notice of the Milk Marketing Board. They offered me a personal sponsorship deal in the form of six free pints of milk a day for the six-week period while my jaw was healing. The reaction of the WRU? No milk. No way. It contravened the amateur regulations. A similar situation arose in 1975 when Knorr Soups offered a much-needed sponsorship for the Welsh Schools Under 15s. The details are not important but Knorr wanted senior players, like myself, to go to supermarkets and shops to publicise the scheme, merely by our presence. Bill Clement, then WRU secretary, immediately went on television to declare the scheme illegal. The Welsh Schools had not asked their permission to accept the sponsorship and, anyway, players should not be used to endorse products. Knorr were kicked out of rugby.

A week later the WRU announced that they were seeking sponsors for the sum of £100,000 for the Welsh Cup. It seems that there is one law for the authorities and another for the rest of us. The WRU also have much to answer for in their planning of the Centenary Season in 1980. Their aim was to raise as much money as possible in order to pay off their overdraft. The marketing men were brought in, products were endorsed and sold. The WRU really went to town. The only people they seemed to forget in all this were the players. They were not taken into consideration when they planned the centenary fixtures, two of which took place in the early part of the season and used players who had just returned from an arduous Lions tour of South Africa. Yet we were expected to peak and produce high quality performances, not only in those early matches, but once a month for the whole season. The WRU raised money all right. But at what cost. The match that really mattered, of course, was against New Zealand. No wonder they thrashed us. After the Lions tour, no one was fit physically or mentally, there was hardly any adrenalin flowing for us to do ourselves justice against the All Blacks.

I've talked of hypocrisy on many occasions. I think the most outstanding example was the Adidas affair. This supposed scandal of alleged payments by the boot manufacturers caused a tremendous uproar among the authorities. The WRU conducted two inquiries into the allegations and found no evidence to support claims that players were paid to wear Adidas boots. Their next step was to almost immediately negotiate with Adidas for a sponsorship to the sum of £75,000 to supply kit for the Welsh team. Adidas, after being labelled the villains of rugby, suddenly became welcome in the carpeted offices of the WRU. There's a moral in this story somewhere.

The whole question of the authorities' attitude towards players is constantly under scrutiny. So it should be. If there is an underlying discontentment with the way the game is administered it is hardly surprising. Take another example. I'm told that five or six years ago, an idea was submitted to the RFU which would have been enormously beneficial to players. Briefly, the plan entailed staging an annual match at Twickenham (or at Cardiff on alternate years, for the WRU were told of the idea) from which the entire proceeds would go towards underwriting a major insurance scheme to cover all players in the event of injury or death. The project included the setting up of major treatment and specialist care centres throughout the country. The long term plan was to establish medical and treatment facilities at every club in England and Wales. It was a marvellous scheme, and you would have thought that the RFU and/or the WRU would have welcomed it with open arms, particularly as one major drugs company which was run by a Welshman, Don Lewis, offered to pay for a feasibility study of the whole plan. There would have been no cost, no obligation by the authorities, but they turned the offer down. The players, once again, were the victims of the officials' narrow-mindedness.

Perhaps the bungling that exists at higher levels of the game, was one of the reasons why David Lord attempted, in 1983, to launch a professional circus. He did not reckon on any great counterattack from the governing bodies killing off his plan. As we now know, there were other reasons why the Pro. Circus failed – David Lord simply could not obtain the necessary financial backing for the scheme. I first met Lord when I went to Australia in 1981 to play for a World XV against Sydney. A journalist-cum-publisher then, Lord produced the souvenir programme for the match. Perhaps it was here with so many stars from all over the world which first sowed the seeds of his idea for a rugby World Cup.

It is fascinating that he got as far as he did. His ultimate failure to bring it off, I'm sure was welcomed with relief by the International Board member countries. Although they had scorned the whole idea, a World Cup would have been a great threat, not the least being that many national sides would have been reduced to 'B' or 'C' status. I do not know how Lord first embarked on his scheme, or which country he approached first when he sounded out players. What I do know is that he came to Wales in April 1983 and, without wishing to incriminate anyone, his presence sent a wave of anticipation through the leading players. Very few were in a position to resist listening to a project which promised upwards of £95,000 for joining! Lord staged two meetings in Wales, at the Seabank Hotel in Porthcawl. It seems incredible now that these supposedly clandestine meetings went unnoticed. Who says secrets can't be kept in rugby? Members of the Welsh Squad attended – as indeed other national squad players attended similar meetings in their own countries.

Lord's scheme involved teams from New Zealand, Australia, Wales, England, Scotland, Ireland, France and the Rest of the World. He claimed that some players had already provisionally agreed to take part. Even the most sceptical were impressed with his attention to detail and the clear, precise answers he gave to all questions from the Welsh players. In the event, the whole idea collapsed. Rugby's status quo was saved from outside interference. The only good thing, I suppose, that resulted from Lord's idea was that it made the world's rugby authorities sit up and take notice. At least I hope they did! It may mean that one day players will get a better deal.

Characters

Looking back over my career, I am left with the inevitable conclusion that it is impossible to do justice to all the players and people who have, for whatever reason, played a significant part in my life or have left some lasting impression, favourable or otherwise. I fear too that some have not been mentioned at all; their omission is unintentional. They simply have not been included because as with many other items space has not permitted it. I am also sorry that I have not been able to pay tribute to some of the players and characters I have been fortunate enough to meet through rugby. I mention the following, if only to prove my memory is not as bad as some may think.

John Perkins is one of the most maligned characters in Welsh rugby, and never deserved his reputation as a rough, uncompromising player. At his best he is a genuine, completely dedicated forward and one of the few lock forwards who have the ability to dominate a line-out with two-handed jumping. He is not recommended company on a tour of Blaenavon pubs, but I regard Perky as a friend of unfaltering loyalty. The opposition who bleated about his rough-riding in the loose, hardly know the chap. Perky would never do anything that he wouldn't like to have done to him. His play is similar to that of a typical All Blacks front jumper. When he tramples in rucks (he doesn't mountaineer as some have suggested) it doesn't matter who he treads on, friend or foe.

Rodney O'Donnell is the most superstitious person I have ever met. If he treads on a crack in the pavement, he would quickly step off it and walk around it. If he fielded the ball after his opponents had kicked a goal, he would have to throw the ball back over the crossbar first. Rodney would also have to change his hotel room if the room number contained 13 or even if the numbers added up to 13.

In Blöemfontein on one Friday the 13th on the 1980 Lions tour, the players played a joke on him. They drew lines on the carpet outside his room so that he couldn't avoid treading on one. They also put sticky labels with 13 written on them on lift buttons and places where he couldn't avoid touching them. He lost his watch on Friday the 13th. I wouldn't be surprised if the player he attempted to tackle when he broke his neck wore No. 13. I think I was lucky to have met him.

In New Zealand in 1977, *Moss Keane* 'Mossie' got into the habit of setting off fire alarms after he'd had a few drinks. He was also the Judge at the Lions' court sessions and the boys thought it appropriate that he wore a fireman's helmet. We made sure he got one. After the first Test, in Wellington, 'Mossie' drank for 30 hours non-stop. It must have been a record, even for a Lion on tour. The tour manager, George Burrell, eventually decided to put Mossie to bed. By the time George, duty done, had got back to the bar, Mossie was right behind him! Mossie had to leave the training field the next day. Some of the reporters thought it was because of delayed concussion from the NZ Universities match, but we all knew differently. Cheers, Mossie.

Willie Duggan has never managed to overcome the effects of jet-lag. He would surface during the day only to go to training, and then he would go back to bed. Willie only came alive during the evening or late at night. He had the knack of killing the ball in rucks for which he took some frightful tramplings from the opposition's forwards. In one match, in Manawatu (4 June 1977), Doug Rollerson, the Manawatu/Horowhenua captain, trampled him and scrum half Mark Donaldson booted him in the head. The referee, incidentally, was Tom Doocey, who had been the controversial referee of the bloody war between France and Wales at Paris in 1983.

In the second Test at Christchurch on 9 July 1977, Willie really took a pounding. His back was covered with stud marks.

But as he was the only fit No. 8, he had to play four days later against the NZ Maoris. His back was padded with foam – and he went on to the field looking like a parachutist! Willie did not last the match. He received a blow to the only part of him which wasn't padded – his jaw. Jeff Squire replaced him and suffered a hamstring injury, but had to stay on because the Lions had used up all their replacements.

There's never been a dull moment with *Geoff Wheel*. He is another of those players who get very nervous before an international. He managed to get the better of Beaumont every time he played against him, including the infamous 1980 match at Twickenham. Geoff should have gone with the Lions that year. Perhaps to a lesser degree, he suffered the same fate as Peter Wheeler on the 1983 tour. Geoff was also unlucky to have to drop out of the 1977 tour with suspected heart trouble. He had no such problem and carried on playing for Wales, when touring Australia in 1978. It must have been a wrong diagnosis. I'll say this, no one had a bigger heart than Geoff Wheel. He was a tremendous player.

Geoff was terrified of flying – coming back from Edinburgh after the Scotland–Wales match in 1981, he boarded the plane with a glass of brandy in one hand and a valium tablet in the other. When he dropped the valium on the floor, I thought he was going to rip up the seat trying to find it.

In Sydney in 1978 our ground floor hotel bedrooms opened directly on to the swimming pool area. About midnight, I was in bed when I heard a terrible racket outside. I went outside to find out what was happening and saw Geoff the giant hammering a towel to the bottom of his door – intent on stopping all the creepy-crawlies he'd been hearing about from entering his room.

During the 1977 tour *Bobby Windsor* turned up for breakfast with a pink patch on his hair fringe. He had been dyeing his grey patch to match his normal colouring, but on this occasion had made a mistake with the dye – he had used pink instead of black! Until then, no one had realised that Bobby was going grey. Of course I had to let all the boys know, didn't I! 'I'll kill you, if you do' Bobby threatened. 'Too late' said I, 'too late.'

I have no way of knowing whether this is true, but I understand that one of the five 1983 Welsh selectors threatened to resign if any of the other four voted for *David Bishop* to be in the Welsh side. Bishop is an enormously talented scrum-half, and has often been described as Pontypool's ninth forward. Not true. We don't need another forward.

When *Ray Gravell* first played for Wales in 1975, he was the find of the season. He was fast, a hard tackler, a good passer, could break inside or outside, could hand off or dip shoulder and run through an opponent. As his career progressed, he carried the can for Wales using the 'crash' ball. But it wasn't his idea. In fact Grav employed it only because he was told to.

Ray is a strong Welsh Nationalist who is extremely proud to play for Wales. He cares a great deal about other people's opinion of him and gets very nervous before all matches – whether they are internationals or for the Lions. He sings Welsh Nationalist songs in changing rooms before matches and on the 1980 tour to South Africa, I became so used to Grav's singing that I even started to enjoy it by the end of the tour. Before one international during the 1980–81 season, Gravs was suffering from a shoulder injury. He had passed a fitness test the day before but needed his confidence boosting. He asked if I would help him out. 'Shoulder charge me and see if I'm up to it Pricey', he asked as we walked from the Angel Hotel to a nearby cinema. So there we were, in the street, banging into each other like a couple of stags before a rut. Funny people, these rugby players, passers-by must have thought.

Gravs, a great character and a fantastic player, was funny all right. He had a reputation for wanting to talk all night before matches. I used to share rooms regularly with him before internationals. I have always liked my eight hours. The first time, I made a joke about having to share with him. Later, he turned to me and asked: 'Pricey, you don't mind sharing a room with me, do you'?

'No Gravs', I replied.

'You like me don't you Pricey?'

'Yes, Gravs.'

'Your wife likes me, doesn't she?'

'Yes, Gravs – and now for heaven's sake, put out your fag, stop talking, get into bed, and go to sleep.'

Gravs obeyed. The following morning he declared: 'Do you know Pricey, that was the best night's sleep I've ever had before an international'.

When *Bill Beaumont* first joined the Lions in New Zealand in 1977, he came with a reputation as a soft touch. He soon surprised everyone with his effort and commitment. I have never received more weight in the scrum than I did from him.

Phil Orr is a wily old campaigner, but a genuine forward. Phil – along with Bobby Windsor – could justifiably feel hard done by when he was dropped after the first Test in New Zealand , 1977, in favour of Fran Cotton. He had not let himself or the team down since the scrummaging in the first Test was the only aspect of the Lions' play which put the All Blacks under any pressure.

Peter Wheeler came into his own when he replaced Bobby Windsor in the Test team in New Zealand 1977. Although he was not as physically strong as Bobby, he contributed a great deal in the loose. Peter has become one of the world's best hookers. Certainly he should have been included in the 1983 Lions party.

I have played in sides which would never have lost if *Gareth Davies* had been playing. It is extraordinary that he was not considered by the selectors to be among the top four fly-halves in Wales in 1984. Gareth's big, booming kicks would have put pressure on New Zealand – and would have given Wales a better platform against many sides since they dropped him.

Bill Evans was the man who gave me my cauliflower ear. Despite Ray Prosser's prediction that I didn't have the kind of ears to be in danger of getting a 'caulie', one started to form about two months before receiving my first cap. The man responsible for it was Bill Evans, my own team-mate at Pontypool. Bill was then our front jumper, who used to take a low, hard ball, which meant that because the ball was not thrown very high, he had to get in front of his opposite number. It wasn't so much a case of outjumping his man as of beating him to the jump. So Bill almost used to run the two steps down the line-out, where I would bind on him. I didn't have to go to him, he came to me, with the result that if I mistimed the bind he used to bang his hip against the side of my head. This continual pounding started the caulie forming, but it wasn't until a week before the final Welsh trial of 1975 that my ear was badly clouted. It swelled up like a balloon, and had to be drained regularly with a syringe. I was told that in order to treat it properly, I would have to stop playing for about three weeks which was something I could not do because by this time I was fully involved in the Welsh team, with internationals every fortnight and squad sessions in-between. So I just carried on, me and my caulie, with Hefin Jones, the club doctor, aspirating it whenever it became swollen. Eventually, the fluid began to harden, with the result that I now have a real 'blemmer'. Thanks, Bill! My left ear isn't in too good a shape either. This has nothing to do with Bill Evans though. I suffered it, courtesy of Jean-Pierre Bastiat's boot, in the Wales–France match of 1976. The ear was split almost completely in half, the ear remaining attached to my head only thanks to a thin sliver of skin at the back of the ear.

Allan Martin was one of the many players to be discarded too soon, for no valid reason, by Wales. 'Panther' was a classical line-out ball winner, but his contribution to the scrummage was not recognised. He was a better scrummager than he was generally given credit for, and one of the best all-round locks I've played with.

One of *Clive Rowlands'* responsibilities, during his time as chairman of the Welsh selectors, was to help put the players in the right frame of mind at the team meeting on the morning of an international match. It wasn't so much an emotional appeal, more a tirade – and was regarded by the players with mixed feelings. These meetings were usually held in one of the team hotel's larger bedrooms but even so the 'accommodation' was rather cramped by the large numbers, sometimes with over 30 players and officials squashed together like sardines. Some of the players went to great lengths, skulking in corners or hiding behind others to avoid being in Rowlands's direct line of vision.

'Are you with me?' he would roar in his broad West Walian accent. The answer he wanted in unison was, 'Yes, we're with you!' 'What do you want to do?' was another passionate question. If our reply of 'win!' did not cause the windows to rattle and the bedroom door to shake, he would demand us to repeat it until he was satisfied that we really meant it. Presumably Rowlands's logic was the louder we shouted, the more we wanted to win! Understandably, some of the players found this rather embarrassing. It was like being back at primary school or at the pantomime. Even more disconcerting was to be singled out. Several of the lads dreaded it. It wasn't so much playing the straight man, more the yes man. Players don't like acting the stooge in such a childish fashion.

After I had been dropped against Scotland in 1983 and then recalled to play against Ireland, I reckoned it was reasonably certain that I'd be one of Rowlands's fall guys at the team meeting. The boys had pulled my leg over the whole affair, and the expected confrontation between me and the selectors, particularly Rowlands, was almost gleefully anticipated in view of the fact that I had hardly congratulated them for kicking me out in the first place. We duly assembled in a room at the Angel. I found myself at the front, only a few feet from Rowlands. 'I am shaking', he began in a tremulous voice. He wasn't the only one. I could feel the bed I was sitting on shake, as the boys tried to suppress their laughter. 'I am visibly moved', Rowlands went on. Behind him, another selector, vainly trying to choke back his own laughter, had to turn his face away. 'How are you feeling?' Rowlands demanded of one of the players. 'Great!', we all shouted. 'I can't hear you', said Rowlands. 'GREAT!', we bellowed. He then turned to me. The personal touch. Considering that I wasn't feeling particularly well disposed towards any of the selectors at the time, it was absurdly embarrassing to be placed in such a situation. Damn it! I thought, I'm not going to tolerate any more. 'Are you with me?', he asked. I didn't utter a word. The silence, as they say, was deafening.

Ian Stephens Ian 'Ikey' Stephens, the Bridgend loose-head prop, proved himself an ideal tourist, on and off the field during the 1983 Lions' tour of New Zealand. He was desperately unlucky to suffer a knee injury early on. Not many realise just how much of an effort he made to get himself fit. At Waitangi, Bay of Islands, I shared a hotel room with Ikey, and we were supposed to be having a few days' relaxation, away from everything to do with rugby. We had a few opportunities to go on boat trips and the like in the afternoons, but Ikey used every available moment he had trying to strengthen the knee ligaments he had damaged against Southland. Our bedroom was like a gymnasium, as Ikey carried out various tortuous exercises. For three days, he went through leg raises and knee bends like a contortionist. I could have cried for him when, after only five minutes of his first serious training session, his knee finally gave way. It was a cruel blow, particularly after all the work he had put in. The injury ended his tour then and there, and he had to fly home. He was badly missed in every sense.

Index

Index

Index

Index